S... Jenny,

Glad we got a chance to connect. Here's to hope for a brighter future for our children ♡

Rachel

Life in Asymmetry

A hopeful journey over the peaks and valleys of genetic breast cancer.

RAYCHEL KUBBY ADLER

BALBOA.
PRESS

A DIVISION OF HAY HOUSE

Balboa Press books may be ordered through booksellers or by contacting:

Balboa Press
A Division of Hay House
1663 Liberty Drive
Bloomington, IN 47403
www.balboapress.com
1 (877) 407-4847

Because of the dynamic nature of the Internet, any web addresses or
links contained in this book may have changed since publication and
may no longer be valid. The views expressed in this work are solely those
of the author and do not necessarily reflect the views of the publisher,
and the publisher hereby disclaims any responsibility for them.

The author of this book does not dispense medical advice or prescribe the use
of any technique as a form of treatment for physical, emotional, or medical
problems without the advice of a physician, either directly or indirectly. The
intent of the author is only to offer information of a general nature to help
you in your quest for emotional and spiritual well-being. In the event you use
any of the information in this book for yourself, which is your constitutional
right, the author and the publisher assume no responsibility for your actions.

Any people depicted in stock imagery provided by Thinkstock are
models, and such images are being used for illustrative purposes only.
Certain stock imagery © Thinkstock.

Print information available on the last page.

ISBN: 978-1-5043-5880-4 (sc)
ISBN: 978-1-5043-5882-8 (hc)
ISBN: 978-1-5043-5881-1 (e)

Library of Congress Control Number: 2016908793

Balboa Press rev. date: 07/28/2016

For my mom, Dodie, and my sister, Lisa:
I hope I have shared your stories well, and
that other women will get to learn and
benefit from your lives in the same way that I did.

And for my girls, Ruby and Marley, whom
I hope will experience a life of the
unmarred beauty of nature's asymmetry.

"I am persuaded that life, as it is known to us,
is a direct result of the asymmetry of the
universe or of its indirect consequences."
-Louis Pasteur

CONTENTS

AUTHORS NOTE

This book is a work of nonfiction. These stories are real but are drawn from my memory and therefore may not be exactly as others remember them. Some names and identifying characteristics have been changed to protect the privacy of the individuals involved.

injury, Dr. Zanvil proceeded to place my mom's hands on my chest so she could feel me up too.

All was not as grand as I expected with these new appendages. I was the first girl in the fifth grade to get them, a time in life when the last thing I wanted was to stick out. I remember learning to play bridge as a part of our math unit that spring and I was more concerned with making sure my cards covered my chest than in how many trumps I could take that round.

What I had longed for so badly now seemed mostly irritating. They were there to stay though, so I decided to make the most of my mounds, and fortunately, within a year they were coming in handy.

They were a big part of the reason that Marc Rosenblum kissed me when we played spin the bottle at 6th grade science camp, and again two years later, sitting in the gazebo outside the 8th grade graduation dance, when Matt Bloom put his hands under my Gunnysack top and sloppily groped my newly ripe melons.

Slumber parties became the best—a chance to take off our t-shirts and show each other our cool new bras. After watching a VCR movie like *Ghost Busters or Back to the Future*, all the party girls would gather in front of the bathroom mirror, wearing only pajama pants and no tops and chant:

"We must, we must,
We must increase our bust.
The bigger the better,
The tighter the sweater,
The boys are depending on us!"

By high school I had full-fledged *boobs*, and I wore them like badges of honor. Young and firm, they provided a great display in my swim team suit, strapless Junior Prom dress, and my billowing, hippie blouses. For my suitors, they were an amusement park, and I was glad to have them to share. My melons were there for the ride when I lost my virginity. Juiced up on homemade wine coolers, wearing my first lacey bra, Dire Straits "Water of Love" playing in the background, and Tim's crimson hair and matching red condom—it was the perfect setting for a Valentine's Day to remember.

Once collegiate, my breasts were most fully appreciated. It was their most playful time in life. They were described by those lucky enough to get to know them as "stacked," "a nice rack," and, one of my all-time favorite compliments, "a perfect handful." Looking equally great jutting out underneath my UCSC banana slug hoodie or in a push-up bra as they bounced to the rhythm of my funk moves at dance parties, my ta-tas enjoyed this new carefree life. They were even bestowed the nickname "billabongs" for the way they curved around the shaft of the 5-foot bong we enjoyed on the weekends. Those girls were ready to rock.

But like a good college party, busted early for being too big or loud, my booby party was cut short by a quick turn of events.

Suddenly my breasts were bull's-eyes.

We three by the fireplace on Palo Hills Drive. Early 80's.

CHAPTER 1

APPLES

It's not pretty to watch a grown woman beg, especially when she's your big sister, and she's dying, and she's begging you to do something that could have saved her life. But I had no choice. We were in the kitchen of the first house I ever owned in Davis, CA. Around the table, the same one my father had grown up with in Phoenix, Arizona, were myself and my big sister Lisa, who was lying across the table grabbing at my arms like a mad woman, determined to convince me it was time. My husband Mitchel was doing the dishes, trying not to make too much noise and wake our baby daughter Marley sleeping down the hall.

Lisa and I had a unique relationship. Born 16 years before me, Lisa was at times a big sister and at other times my "cool mom." I was Lisa's mini-me in many physical ways—same face, same body shape. People always commented on how much we looked alike when they saw us together. Most picked up that we were sisters but some assumed we were mother and daughter, or that Lisa was my aunt. Without missing a beat, one of us would respond with our go-to story, "twins separated at birth by 16 years." But what was even more striking was the ways in which we shared other less genetic characteristics like having the same laugh and weird sense of humor, and a shared passion for music, cuddling, and rubbing feet. I loved our sameness.

When my mom was with us, people really got confused. In our three silhouettes there was a surprising symmetry. My father, who went by "Pop" my whole life, had a favorite aphorism, "The apple doesn't fall very far from the tree," which rang true for the female line of our family and I was proud of it. The same phrase however could make me cringe when Pop used it to imply I was like him in some way.

Yet when my mother and then my sister got diagnosed with breast cancer within six months of each other, it did cross my mind that I might be next, but I let it go. Although a laboratory just down the road at UC Berkeley was coming close to cloning the first breast cancer gene, it would be another year before the public was aware of it. Plus, it was no great stretch to find a cancer culprit in the rays coming from the microwave my mom used to cook most of our meals, or the water we had been drinking our whole lives in Los Altos Hills.

It wasn't until Lisa found her second breast cancer tumor eight years later and was urged to undergo genetic testing that our understanding of the significance really hit home. Recent research had identified two genetic mutations, which put carriers at very high risk for early onset breast and ovarian cancer. Due to her multiple occurrences of breast cancer, the first at the young age of 36, Lisa was a prime suspect for this condition, and given my mom's and my sister's diagnosis, it was no big leap to assume I was next.

From the day Lisa got a positive result, it became her number one priority to make sure I got tested.

As I sat at the kitchen table looking at Lisa I realized that her pleading held even graver meaning. She had recently learned that her cancer had metastasized to her spine and there were a few spots in her lungs. Lisa was clear that she could no longer save herself; so she made it her prerogative to make a difference for me. She was trying to protect me like only a loving sister could.

Closing my eyes, and rubbing my hands against the kitchen table, I could feel the stories of those who had sat at this same table in the grains of wood. I could hear the sobs of my grandmother, crying at the table when she returned from the cemetery after putting her not-even-three- year-old son to rest. I could almost see my mother sitting next to me with her lunch of salad and a quesadilla, the phone to her ear as Lisa told her the news that she also had cancer.

The sound of Mitchel turning on the garbage disposal pulled me out of my thoughts. Marley was now far enough in her sleep cycle that the noise wouldn't wake her. When I looked up at him he shot back a look that let me know he appreciated how challenging all of this was for me—being pregnant and having babies without having my own mother around, Lisa being so ill, the pressure to do something about my own risk, and the undeniable implications all this would have on Marley and the new baby girl brewing in my belly.

I looked up at Lisa, who was still leaning across the table as if the closeness of our faces might lend urgency to her pleading. It is true that her pale blue eyes were like a mirror into my own--the lines in her face telling a story of what was ahead for me.

Tears flooded my eyes and I blinked hard trying to clear them, yet through this cloudy vision I saw my sister from a new perspective—her features morphing into something asymmetrical to mine; close, but not an exact reflection.

I would have different choices to make. The future was not predetermined by my genetics alone. There were several options and infinite possible outcomes.

Pop was right, our apples were similar, but he didn't account for what happened after each apple fell to the ground. My apple might land close to the tree, but there was no telling where it would roll to after.

I could change the course of my apple.

Lisa and me before her wedding in1986.

Mom, Lisa and me (right to left) near the Golden Gate Bridge 1990.

My big sis and me (Early 90's) on the waters of Lake Canandaigua, NY. I believe this shot by Bruce Brannon won an award at Kodak where he worked.

I don't ever remember realizing we were so close until we already were. Being with her was magic. We came from the same stock, were cut from the same silk. Indeed, we were two peas in a pod. She understood me like nobody else could and connected with me in a way that let me know how very deeply she loved me. Lying side-by-side on her queen bed, headphones streaming The Grateful Dead and Joni Mitchell into my ears, holding her hand, I wanted to stay there forever. She was my heart home.

There were more awkward events during these middle years. My Bat Mitzvah was probably one of the lowest of the lows. There I was, pasty skin covered in acne, hormones raging, and I had to parade in front of all my family and a few friends speaking a foreign language, and act as though it were the most glorious of moments. I can barely look at the photos from that day, my braces-filled smile glaringly bright and uncomfortable. I do remember being happy with the rainbow Jelly Belly centerpieces my mom made as table decorations, and that Matt Martin asked me to slow dance to Wham's hit "Careless Whisper."

My self-esteem wasn't much better a year and a half later when I was a bridesmaid at my sister's wedding. The rest of the wedding party was in their late twenties and had hips and breasts that filled out the sheer fabric of the peach-colored bridesmaid dresses. I had to stand by Lisa's side wearing a bridesmaid dress that looked on my hipless waist like a potato sack, while the other bridesmaids looked like mermaids, and I had to watch and smile as this stranger took my best friend 3,000 miles away to be a Rochester, New York housewife. I wished all the time that Lisa was at my side. I knew she was the one that could best help me face the challenges of teenage life. She would offer me answers without judgment.

Luckily, my own intimate relations were heating up, which helped take my mind off of missing my sister. As my emotional terrain began to improve, my physical landscape also continued to blossom. Although things were looking up in this realm, for good and for bad, it seemed that life, and my body, were taking on new dimensions.

The newspaper clipping announcing my dad's run for City Councilman and my birth. I was supposed to be a tax baby (April 15, 1972) but ended up coming early.

First family photo (1972)

An early photo of we three. I am the baby, Lisa has the long hair and my mom is lighting candles. Check out the metal high chair I was rocking.

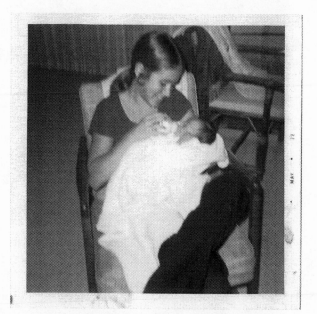

First photo of Lisa and me that that I can find.

Lisa and me at Stanford Family Camp, CA.

CHAPTER 3

BONGOS

College life suited me well. I loved the opportunities around me, enjoyed my first experience of being on my own, and the surroundings at UC Santa Cruz could not be any better. Mountains meeting ocean yielded the best kind of playground I could imagine. My classes were stimulating and provocative and the community of people I called my friends was warm, engaging, progressive and passionate. I developed newfound loves for backpacking, stargazing, ocean kayaking and surfing. I traded in my parking space on campus for a Rockhopper mountain bike.

My classes were blowing my mind. It was great to pick what subjects I was interested in, and the level of learning was engaging and challenging. The Physics of Chemistry was one of my favorites. The teacher was a strange combination of wacky and tough. She would come into class, an Amazon at 6'1", dressed in a hand-woven blouse creation, some spirited African print pants and one of her signature metal based jewelry pieces wrapped around her neck, weighing down her ears, or dangling from her wrist. Before class started she would stand on top of a stepping stool so she could be fully viewed above the countertop crowded with beakers and Bunsen burners and ask us to identify the elements she was wearing that day before we could move on with our lessons. This class came way before the era of Harry Potter and Hogwarts magic seminars, but it functioned in the same way. We spent the hour and ten minutes blowing things up or trying to change the color or form of some mystery substance with our lab partners.

I was focused on getting a good grade in the class because I really wanted to take a Biology course that had chemistry as a prerequisite. When the professor offered us extra credit to do a research project on a modern chemistry issue, I read an article about Mary-Claire King, a geneticist at Berkeley, the other UC, just down the road, who was doing research into a gene that might cause cancer. It announced that together with her team of scientists, Ms. King had found conclusive evidence linking DNA markers on a certain chromosome with an inherited flaw in a gene dubbed BRCA1. Her finding would change the face of breast and ovarian cancer, and, unbeknownst to me, would also prove groundbreaking for my future.

With all the new excitement of college, I didn't go home often. But one evening my mom called on a Thursday, I remember because I had just been at the Santa Cruz farmer's market. I was surprised that she was calling me only two days after we had just had our ritual Sunday afternoon check-in.

"Hi Honey," my mom said. "How's your day goin'?"

"Fine mom. I had class this afternoon and now I'm heading to swim. What's up?"

"Um, well, I didn't ask you when we talked on Sunday if you were coming home for Debra's bat mitzvah," she said more like a statement than a question. "You could do some laundry and I can take you to Gemco to get anything you need for your room."

"Oh yeah, I remember you saying something about that. Let me see if I can find a ride and I'll let you know."

"Okay sweetie. It'll be great to see you," my mom said, her voice filled with a pleading mixed with sadness. *She must be missing me.*

I could tell something was off with Mom the minute I got to the door because she didn't come down to greet me.

"The inside garage door is open," she called out through the whole-house intercom. "Come in that way, honey."

The inside garage door, I thought to myself. The garage was pretty much only used to store extra frozen items, bikes, sports equipment, and a workbench. The two-car garage didn't actually house any cars, they were all lined up outside on the driveway--Pop's Chrysler convertible, Mom's Oldsmobile station wagon, and my friend's Saab that I had borrowed for the drive up from Santa Cruz.

Shakti, the black lab my parents had taken in when my sister moved to New York, ran around the porch to stick her nose through the slats of the banister and greet me. I smiled back at her, glad someone was excited to see me.

When I got upstairs, Mom was sitting at her desk at the edge of the kitchen. She waited until I was right in front of her to get up and give me a hug, but as she did, any perceived weirdness from not coming to the door fell away. We moved into regular banter about my classes and roommates and her weaving and tennis. She seemed tired, like she'd been missing her daily 20-minute "power naps."

"I'm glad you came home," Mom said, her voice deeper than typical. "I wanted to get to talk with you in person."

My body suddenly had a fight or flight reaction. I went into full defense mode. Our family hardly ever "talked." I mean we talked a lot, but not about our feelings or emotional life. The last time my mom "asked me to talk" was to tell me that she needed some help with doing her taxes and balancing her checkbook, Mom's roundabout way of letting me know that she and Pop were breaking up. Talking meant there was an issue. Something was wrong.

"I found out I have a little lump in my breast. They saw something on a routine mammogram so they followed up with a needle biopsy."

I tugged at my hoodie trying to find words for this. "Oh. Man. That really sucks, Mom. I'm so sorry. What did they say after the biopsy?" I asked, bracing myself for what was next. She wouldn't have brought me home or started this talk unless it was bad.

"They said it's cancer."

My face must have reacted to that word because Mom went right into mom mode, trying to make it all okay.

"It's minor, honey. You don't have to have that worried face. They're going to do a lumpectomy in a few weeks and cut the little bit out. A few weeks later I'll start some kind of treatment, but they haven't decided just what yet. It'll be fine."

Mom really did sound sure that all would be okay, but I was still stuck on the word "treatment." I said it a few times in my head—as I'd done as a child, repeating words like "chair" or "flower" over and over again in my head until the word started to sound meaningless. I hadn't been exposed to cancer before, so I didn't know much about the various treatments. The only image I could conjure up was an old lady wearing a scarf because she lost all her hair.

I looked up at my mom for a moment wondering what she would look like bald. She just didn't seem like someone who would get sick. When I was a child she hadn't tolerated sickness in our house. I only have two memories of being sick as a kid. Once, when I was about 3 or 4 and I spiked a high fever, Mom laid me in my towel and turned on the television. I was embarrassed that Mr. Rogers on the television could see my bare bottom through the tubes.

The other memory is when Mom sent me over to Jen Chu's house for a "chicken pox party" when Jen and her brother David had active pocks. Mom said she thought it best to plan out getting the chicken pox than to wait for it to happen at what might be a less convenient time.

"They put me at Stage II," Mom said. "They said the tumor is small and hasn't moved beyond the area where it was first growing. From the mammogram it didn't seem there was any lymph node involvement. If they treat the area," she said, "all will be well."

My mom lived by all kinds of these credos. Her favorite was, "I believe in the sun even when it rains." One piece of art hung in her bathroom, a pencil drawing I made in the first grade of a sun shining bright through lots of raindrops and clouds. She would be okay. The sun would shine.

Our conversation lasted less than five minutes and then we went on with my short visit home without any further conversations about her health. As I was arranging my bags and laundry in the back of the car for my return trip on Sunday, Mom leaned in through the passenger window looking very calm. I was glad she wasn't worried though I found it a bit odd. I was more a mess than either of my parents it seemed. I didn't want my mom to have cancer. This wasn't part of the story.

"I'll see you Thursday then," I said, "for your appointment." I meant for my voice to say that as a statement, but my mom dove right in and took the raise in my voice to indicate I had asked if I should come or not.

"No need to do that, Honey. It's a quick in and out thing. You should stick to your classes. Really."

Pop, standing behind her, caught my glance but shrugged his shoulders. I wasn't even sure what he was doing there, but it seemed he had come back to help her through whatever her treatment might be. There was nothing any of us could do when my mom stated a plan. It had always been that way. She had the final word in our family.

Lisa got the same response from my parents when she asked if she should come out. "It's okay, Lisa," Mom said. "We know you have a lot going on."

Lisa's life was very full. She was mom to Dylan who at 2 years old wanted to toddle his way into every nook and cranny of the world he could find. Climbing, digging, building, he was always busy and kept Lisa on her toes. She had also recently given birth to her second son, Elliott, and on top of it all doing her job as the director of a mental health facility while on maternity leave.

"Okay, maybe I can come out a little later," Lisa said, "when you're doing your treatments. You can see Elliott and I can help out however you need."

Joel offered to fly out for the surgery but was turned away as well. Pop took my mom to the lumpectomy appointment and called me when they got home, saying the procedure had gone well. Then, with no changes to our weekly phone calls and no breaks from her twice-weekly tennis dates, Mom did eight rounds of chemo in eight weeks. She powered her way through cancer like she did so many things in life. Our family followed her lead and didn't think much about it either.

Diagnosed at 62, Mom was in a relatively common age bracket to be finding a small breast tumor. There were no red flags. Breast cancer became a short blip in our lives.

Or at least for the next nine months, that was what we all decided to believe.

CHAPTER 4

BOMBSHELLS

All my memories of Lisa include her having big breasts. Of the women I knew in our family, Lisa was the biggest breasted. Both Mom and Pop claim their mom's were voluptuous—so perhaps it skipped a generation. Sure, I have seen pictures of her as a baby and young girl, riding her bike down Waverly St. in Sunnyvale, when she was too young to have breasts, but since I was born when Lisa was a teenager, she already had boobs when we met. After having her second child, Lisa's breasts crossed over the line from where they were adult toys, to being all about providing sustenance and comfort for her children. Her breasts were meant to provide—milk, a pillow, or a snuggle. There were so many ways that Lisa's life had changed due to becoming a mom. For one thing, Lisa got very little sleep. Seems babies have the worst issues between the hours of 3 to 5 am—and Elliott, her second, had a lot of tummy troubles. Lisa and Bruce tried every trick in the book: bicycle his legs, give him a light abdominal massage, and give him a bath. By day, Lisa spent all of her time tending to their diapers, meals and socialization, and had very little time for herself.

Lisa told me that sometimes, to get a few moments to herself, she would go to the bathroom and just hang out there. Sometimes she would take a rejuvenating shower, or just sit on the toilet and read. Anything to get a short breather and get grounded.

But when she called to tell me about her latest shower there was no relaxation in that hot water.

"I was soaping myself up, you know, running my hands over my body to lather it up, but then I felt something. It felt like a welt at first, you know, outside my skin, but as I touched it more it felt like a small pebble. It's to the outside of my left breast."

My throat started to feel swollen. I was scared by what I was hearing but didn't want to give that away. "I'm sure it was nothing Lis. Didn't you say a few weeks ago that you had mastitis? It's probably just a plugged duct or something," I said, not really knowing what I was talking about but wanting to say something.

"I know. That's what Bruce said too. But I swear I keep feeling it over and over again. There's something there." I knew what Lisa needed right then was for me to talk her down. She had a habit of catastrophizing and I was the one who could keep her from spiraling too far out. I lived through Lisa having amaxophobia (fear of being in a car) before I learned to drive.

"It's gonna be okay, Lis, really. You need to slow down and breathe."

Over the next week Lisa felt the same spot throbbing every time she nursed Elliott. It got so irritating she had to stop nursing all together. Yet even with these strange symptoms and my mom's recent diagnosis, Lisa was not thinking about breast cancer. None of her friends had breast cancer. Not even many of her friends' moms.

But the pain could not be tolerated anymore, even without nursing, so Lisa made an appointment with her Ob/Gyn, who, after a brief palpitation of her breast, sent Lisa immediately to have an MRI and a needle biopsy.

I was the first call that Lisa made after she and Bruce left the doctor's office with the results. She started the conversation the way I am sure that many other difficult discussions have begun: "Are you sitting down?"

I wasn't yet, but I could tell I should be. I pulled at the telephone line to see if I could uncoil it a bit to reach the kitchen breakfast bar area, and had a seat on one of the stools.

"I have a cancerous mass in my left breast," she said. I could hear the gargle of all the tears and mucus in her throat. It made me feel so far away from her.

I stared around the empty living room of our dorm apartment. These hard knocks were not the lessons I expected to learn in college. It seemed impossible that a healthy, 36-year-old, new mom could get breast cancer, and even more impossible that it could be my sister. I was still getting used to having a mom that was a cancer survivor.

"Oh, Lis. I don't even believe this. I mean, it's crazy. Really? They know its cancer? How did this happen?" I shot off all these questions even though I wasn't expecting her to answer me. "Do you want me to come there and help?"

Hearing these words come out of my mouth I cringed. These were the same questions we had been asking my mom less than a half a year before.

"I'm not even sure what the treatment will be," she said. "I've got the baby to think about. It all seems so surreal."

I realized that in the last few months the word "treatment" had developed a context--there would likely be radiation, and maybe chemo. Lisa would most likely lose her thick beautiful hair.

Before hanging up we made a plan to talk in a few days.

"You'll be out of school for summer break in a few weeks," Lisa said. "Maybe you can come here for a week and we can see some movies and get our toenails painted."

"I can babysit," I said, "I would love to be with the boys. You and Bruce can have some romantic evenings out. Whatever. I'm your girl." I felt like a cheerleader giving Lisa a personal pep rally when all I think we both wanted to do was to fall into each other's arms and let out huge sobs of sadness.

"Thanks Ray Ray, I know you are," Lisa said. "I feel ya sista."

I could tell by the way she said "sista," in our usual silly sister slang, that she was smiling. This brought a little comfort to the unsettling content of the conversation, and we said good-bye.

"I'm calling Mom next," she said in closing. "Wish me luck!"

My mom didn't take the news as well as I did. Deep into her own treatment by then, Mom had recently begun suffering from radiation burns on her skin. She couldn't stand the thought that Lisa would endure the suffering of breast cancer—although at the same time Mom would never admit that she was in pain. The worst possible situation for my mom was that one of her children was in pain. "I wish it were me," my mom would always say when I was a kid and skinned my knee or had laryngitis.

Lisa took on her diagnosis like a warrior. She began interviewing doctors and asking them tough questions, like why they chose their profession. For Lisa their answer was just as important as what credentials they held. She picked Dr. Crowford, one of the most preeminent breast cancer surgeons in Rochester, because he admitted that in medical school, while watching his sister be treated for cancer, he realized that he didn't want to be a "jock doc," but instead to make a difference in cancer treatment.

Lisa's doctors suggested a different treatment plan from my mom. The cancer was deep within her breast tissue, closer to the chest wall and would require a full mastectomy to remove. My mom, pop and Bruce sat together at Highland Hospital for about 12 hours, the longest amount of time they had ever spent together.

Lisa's first chemo was on the day of the Oklahoma City bombing. She called me from the infusion chair to ask if I'd heard the news. It struck me that Lisa was more concerned for the strangers in Oklahoma than the devastation of what was happening in that chair.

Unknown to us, at the same time as Lisa's diagnosis, Myriad Genetics had cloned the BRCA2 gene. What we should have considered was that perhaps the sameness we shared on the outside, might also affect who we were on the inside. Yet somehow none of us connected the dots at that point. It would be another eight years before we would learn about this new version of symmetry we shared.

So I went on with my life, doing the things that one does when their sister and mother are breast cancer survivors. My pom-poms became cheerleaders for the Pink Ribbon team. I walked 60 miles in the *Avon Breast Cancer 3-Day*, participated yearly in the *Relay for Life*, ran in every *Komen Race for the Cure* that came to my area, and fundraised thousands of dollars for breast cancer through these events. Every time I bought stamps I paid a wee bit extra to aid breast cancer research. I was a walking, talking supporter of all things breast cancer prevention. And I planned to keep it that way, always about others, never about me.

I hatched a plan to be the one to outrun breast cancer.

Mitchel and Me during the Avon Breast Cancer 3-Day walk. Day one, we hadn't even started walking yet and day two, probably the hardest of them all!

CHAPTER 5

GIRL HUMPS

My rump was beautifully curved, full, well defined, athletic, and had a strong smile line. Crowning its glory was a tattoo sitting on my sacral chakra, Swadhisthana, the lowest chakra at the base of the spine, which governs reproduction, creativity, joy and enthusiasm. If feeling especially cocky, I might call my rear end a work of art. So after so much focus on my upper assets over the years, it was a breath of fresh air to find a man who appreciated the curves of my rear as well.

Mitchel was that man. He was butt boy. Not at all in a gay way, though I wasn't so sure at first. We met through a shared summer job, taking teenagers from the Bay Area to Israel for the summer. One night, early in the trip, I had seen Mitchel out on the streets of Jerusalem sitting at a little outdoor café table with another good looking young man. The closeness of their faces suggested an intimacy that I translated into romance. I was, however, wrong on that call, and would soon be very glad that I was.

While I thought Mitchel was cute, he thought I would make a great counterpart at work. Over the years since, I have pressed him to admit that he also thought I was cute, but he has held out that it wasn't his intention to make me his wife when he asked me to apply for the job where he would be my boss.

Within three months of working together we were officially "on" as a couple. Our courtship was fast paced and intense since the stakes on our viability as a couple were higher than usual. Worried about lawsuits in the aftermath of the Clarence Thomas incident, Mitchel went to seek the Rabbi's approval. Naturally, he got big thumbs-up and a *mazal tov* from the Rabbi who was full of *nachas* (joy) to see two young Jewish professionals falling in love under his roof. For a Rabbi, the luck of such a happy match is like a notch on the belt, only, in this instance it is more like another knot of the special twined and knotted fringes known as *tzitzit* attached to the four corners of a *talit*, the Jewish prayer shawl.

Quickly my parents grew to love this sweet guy from New York and how he cared for me. They folded Mitchel into our family and gave him the West Coast kin he was missing. Though they dare not say it, I know both of my parents were secretly relieved that this was the guy I picked out of the cast of characters that had paraded through my love life over the years. Smart, Jewish, handsome, kind, and funny, my parents saw in Mitchel the perfect potential son-in-law.

Fortunately and unfortunately, Mitchel and I were also brought together by our shared experience as the children of breast cancer survivors. For his mom Marcia, breast cancer was just another issue to add to her laundry list of health challenges. Four years before we met, Mitchel's mom suffered a massive aneurysm in her brain leaving her permanently paralyzed on the right side of her face and body. A few years later, doctors found a tumor in Marcia's breast and she had a single sided mastectomy without reconstruction. Knowing Marcia was a reminder that bad things happen to good people, and that life was not equitable. This was a woman with a hard knocked life.

Too early in our relationship Mitchel and I had already had a heart-to-heart conversation about our family history, and how unfortunate it was to have so much breast cancer in our genetic pool. Also, at the ripe age of 22, it was a first to be talking about the progeny I would create with someone. I dropped deeper into my love for this man.

As Mitchel and I joined forces, and began to take on the world together, this included going head to head with breast cancer together. Pink became the new black. We shopped for pink friendly products; got involved with our local chapter of Y-Me, a support group for young women with breast cancer; and hung a plastic breast self-exam (BSE) instruction card over the shower head.

It was simple:

1. Use the pads of the three middle fingers.
2. Move your fingers slowly in small coin-sized circles.
3. Use three different levels of pressure to feel all of your breast tissue.
4. Start in the armpit and work down to the bottom of the bra line.
5. Move one finger-width toward the middle and work up to the collarbone.
6. Repeat until you have covered the entire breast.

Sadly, the reminder to practice BSE fell on idle hands, and it was not only that little piece of plastic that was reminding me. My mom asked me if I was checking my breasts, as did my sister, and Mitchel. The worst was when a doctor asked. I felt like a delinquent kid who hadn't practiced their instrument. *No, no BSE doctor. Sorry.*

Nobody seemed to understand the fear that took over every time I touched my breasts. They were rife with bumps and I couldn't tell one hump from the next lump for the life of me. I quickly came to realize I couldn't live like this, knowing how high my risk was, but not able to take matters into my own hands, quite literally, and do BSE.

One afternoon, after yet another feeble attempt, I decided it was time to step things up and let a more reliable method of surveillance take over. I made a call and set an appointment with Women's health for a clinical breast exam.

Dressed in a crinkly paper gown, my body was already tense thinking about the stirrups and speculum that I knew would be coming. The Ob/Gyn bustled into the room; her face haggard and hair frizzled in a way that made it seem she'd been up all night waiting for a prodromal labor to take hold so she could deliver a baby. My anxiety level doubled when, without looking up from my chart, she stated, "I see here you have quite a family history of breast cancer."

"Uh huh," I barely squeaked, my heart filling my throat.

"Your sister was very young," she continued.

"Uh huh," I stammered again. My mind was screaming, *Do you need to remind me?* It was so loud in my head that this was all I could get out.

"Hopefully you're practicing regular breast self-exam," the doctor said in a tone that took me back to my childhood piano teacher asking if I had practiced daily. Shame took over my thoughts as I tried to find some way to validate why I had not. Impossible to explain to anyone without my family history how the fear of getting cancer was enough to overwhelm my ability to do the very thing that could save me. However it appeared she was not looking for a response because the doctor kept right on talking.

"You should really consider getting your first mammogram soon. The recommendation in high-risk cases like yours is to get one ten years before your closest relative found her first lump."

My brain fixated on the words "high-risk" that had just escaped the doctor's mouth. I knew my family's track record, but hearing it said out loud was like being slapped with a label. I was being categorized now and there were "recommendations" that I should be following.

I began calculating in my head. Lisa was 36 when she found her first lump. Ten years earlier meant now.

Suddenly the breast cancer bull's-eye moved front and center...I was the next target.

CHAPTER 6

CALI GIRLS

My blond locks, bronze skin and buxom breasts were the visual parts of my California persona, but my roots ran much deeper. I grew up in Silicon Valley at the boom of the tech industry, declared myself a vegetarian at the age of 12, and found my center on the craggy cliffs and sandy shores of the Pacific Ocean. I was a California Girl through and through.

I didn't quite realize how much of my identity was tied up in this place until I fell in love with an East Coaster. As we were getting to know one another, Mitchel and I enjoyed exploring all the ways in which our identities were shaped by where we grew up. We loved our differences, although I was secretly relieved that while Mitchel missed the brilliant colors of an East Coast fall, he really did feel more himself on the West Coast. So when he began to talk about applying to graduate school and of having the chance to share the East Coast part of himself with me, I wanted to sink into my California pedigree even more. Here was where my parents lived and the community I'd collected. All the places and people and roads I had known my whole life. I didn't want to budge.

Yet the applications, brochures, and promotional materials began arriving at our bungalow in Albany, CA, in a steady stream. Picking up the mail, I would glance at the glossy covers, boasting

happy-looking, preppy people sitting on a sprawling lawn in front
of some large, imposing white building. A few books would be
strewn about the people engaged in what appeared to be very
stimulating conversation. The content and focus of the mailers
were mixed. Some invited prospective students to high profile
MBA programs. Others encouraged the pursuit of various types
of doctoral degrees in Psychology: PhD, PsyD, MED.

After only two years together I already knew that any of
those options would pan out fine for Mitchel. He's one of those
rare breeds who could put his mind to anything in the universe
and be successful. I hadn't yet encountered a sport he wasn't
great at, a hobby he hadn't refined, or a topic he wasn't fairly well
versed to discuss. Mitchel was what I would call an all-arounder
a remarkable accomplishment for a kid whose father never learned
to read past the 4th grade level and who credits his strong value
system on TV shows like *The Facts of Life, Family Ties, and Diff'rent
Strokes*.

But the fact of our life was that the geographic locations of
each program were strewn about. Brochures from Colorado,
Oregon, and Washington were all contenders. And then there
was Rutgers, smack dab in the middle of New Jersey.

There was no doubt that I had some unfounded preconceived
notions about people in New Jersey, and really all the East Coast.
A majority of Mitchel's friends from his youth had become doctors
or lawyers or worked in finance. Most were already married, some
with kids, and lived in big houses in the suburbs. His sister, Jill,
lived in a ritzy, Jewish suburb of New Jersey with two kids, a
mortgage, and two leased vehicles. I had never even heard of a car
lease. And I would bet that "compost" was not in their vocabulary.
How would I fit in?

"I'll go anywhere but New Jersey," I blurted out one night
when Mitchel brought up Rutgers over our dinner plates of tofu
and roasted root vegetables. "It's too far from home."

"*Your* home you mean," Mitchel said.

"You're right. It's true. I'm being closed-minded, I know. But you left the East Coast because you knew it was better out here, right? Why go back?"

As soon as I asked the question, I knew the answer.

In recent years, Mitchel's mom's cancer had metastasized and they didn't give her much more time to live. We could be less than an hour from her if we lived near Rutgers. It would also be a chance for me to live near the rest of his side of the family and get to know them better, as well as his friends from life before we met. But I was wary of what might happen if he attended graduate school somewhere I didn't want to live permanently. He would make contacts there; have colleagues to support and to be supported by. It would be hard to leave.

I felt bad that I wasn't thinking like a team player, but my feelings were deep set. Mitchel was miffed and disappointed, and rightly so. I made it a priority to commit to thinking it over and not making a rash decision based on fear and inflexibility. For the first time in my life, I engaged a therapist to help me think it all through and understand where my resistance was based. Along the way I was able to see additional benefits of the move. At the top of the list was the opportunity to be much closer to Lisa, Joel, and my nephews, all of whom lived in Rochester, New York.

When Lisa had her first breast cancer strike in 1994, her sons Dylan and Elliott were five and two, respectively. I was in my last year of college at the time, without much money or flexibility and was not much help to her from 3,000 miles away. It killed me that Lisa had managed cancer and sat through hours of chemo without me by her side.

The idea of being near Lisa again, and to have a chance to really be Auntie to my nephews, was a strong pull. I had always wished Lisa would get smart and bring her family to California, but since that wasn't happening, New Jersey offered an option to be closer.

The final and most relevant consideration was that I was in love with Mitchel. This was a chance to learn more about him and strengthen our relationship.

By summer's end our boxes were packed and we had a U-Haul filling party for all our friends and family to come and say good-bye. It was all I could muster to offer a weak cheer of "New Jersey or Bust" out the U-Haul window as we pulled away from the curb and began our journey.

The first leg of our journey was only to my mom's place 100 miles south. We decided that before moving across country and starting a new life, a big trip was in store. So we dropped our stuff in Mom's storage unit and flew halfway around the world to Indonesia for a month-long trek. Partway through the trip we ventured by boat to Gili Air, a small island (gili) off the coast of Lombok, which resides just east of Bali in the string of 17,508 gilis, the largest archipelago in the world. Indonesia, by my accounts, is also the most spiritually whole, aesthetically astounding and romantic places I have been. The Buddhist custom in Bali of giving thanks every morning by making alters of incense, flower buds, rice and coins, which fill the streets with color and the sweet smell of Nag Champa, was one of my favorite experiences. I loved the lush green carpet of rice patties dotted with the stark white of egrets finding breakfast there, and the mists encircling the mountains left me wondering what was hidden above. And the night's air, full of jasmine and wafts of warm peanut sauce, filled me with comfort. There was magic afoot.

One evening, as we sat on the edge of that island, watching the sun dip into the sea, we talked about our bright future. Our eyes locked for a bit longer than usual and an electrifying energy moved between us.

Mitchel broke the silence.

"I think we should get married," he said, ever the egalitarian. "I feel like, if you are willing to go to the one place that you said you wouldn't go, well that sounds to me like you're making a commitment to forever. Right?"

Not having the words to respond but unable to contain my excitement I blurted out, "Yes! Yes! I'm screaming yes inside." And in one very sweet moment in life, I replaced my "never" with a wholehearted "forever."

CHAPTER 7

PANCAKES

The Game of Life really expands exponentially when you get married, especially when the couple plans to have children together, which Mitchel and I hoped to do. On a wedding planning trip to California in March, we met with Rabbi Barenbaum, who would be marrying us in July. We went over some details of the service but the primary purpose of our meetings was to talk about our relationship, what we hoped for our family, and what the commitment we were about to make meant to each of us. It felt wonderful to share our love story with the Rabbi since he had been an integral part of our beginnings. Mitchel and he reminisced about their conversation when we started dating and Mitchel was hoping for the Rabbi's blessing on our relationship.

Rabbi Barenbaum also asked us what we knew about our Tay Sachs carrier status. Tay Sachs is a genetic disease that is prevalent in the Eastern European Jewish (Ashkenazi) heritage that Mitchel and I were both a part of. Screening for Tay Sachs carriers was one of the first great successes of the emerging field of genetic counseling and diagnosis and it was now close to eradicated. Bringing two Tay Sachs carriers together raised the hazard of creating a child who could suffer from a disease that causes death by the age of four. Our decision to tie the knot was not just about joining our love; it was also about combining our genetic pools.

Pop had lost two siblings to the disease, leaving him an only child, so I had heard a lot about this disease early on. The good Jews we were, Mitchel and I had talked about this pretty early in our courtship. I felt it was an important part of sharing what I was bringing to the relationship. Thankfully, Mitchel knew there was no Tay Sachs in his line of the family, so we didn't need to be tested ourselves. I wondered if this would still be a concern when the children I hoped to have with Mitchel were ready to have children.

Though it was a relief to not bring this gene to the marital table, we did come with some pretty heavy baggage in terms of our family health histories. We talked with Rabbi Barenbaum about the struggles our mothers had each endured with their health, and also about Lisa's breast cancer. We also shared our sadness that Mitchel's mom Marcia would not be able to make it to our wedding, and discussed how we hoped to honor and remember her at the service.

Marcia had gotten much sicker the past few months and around the start of the new year it became clear that she would not be able to make it to our wedding. On our weekly visits to see her, taking her to her favorite strip mall Chinese restaurant, we shared with her our wedding plans, the guest lists and songs that we would play. We told her that we would put a candle under the *huppah*, the traditional Jewish wedding canopy, for her so that she would be with us. She was thrilled to know that we would be together and that Mitchel would be a husband and father some day and so glad that we would go through life together.

When we left the Rabbi's quarters I felt elated to be getting married, to begin this next leg of the journey with Mitchel, and to create a family.

There was a long list of things that needed to happen in the final weeks before our wedding—check in with the band on how our dance was coming along, give a final count to the caterer, have a pre-wedding photo shoot, and finalize hair, dress fitting, and mani/pedi appointments. Also on my list were less festive things to do. I figured it smart to mix the fun of cake tasting with the more mundane but necessary, like a dental cleaning and the dreaded trip to the Ob/Gyn. With my upcoming marriage my humps would became "assets," part of the dowry of my body and soul that I offered my husband at our wedding, so it seemed fitting that before we tied the knot, I should do something to assure the family jewels were fit for marriage.

I was filled with a feeling of dread for a few days before my mammogram appointment—wishing I could continue in the vein of ignorance is bliss a little longer. But I knew ultimately if there was anything to know, I wanted to know it as soon as possible. When the day came, Mitchel went off to class, wishing me well, and I got in my red Honda Civic and drove to the Clifton Breast Imaging Center.

Walking in the office, I already felt like a freak being a California girl living in New Jersey. As I stepped through the door and toward the check-in desk I scanned the crowd and felt even more misplaced. I was an outlier in that room, not anywhere near the 40 to 80-year-old demographic of women who should get a mammogram every few years. I felt the eyes of the other ladies-in-waiting checking me out, wondering with both intrigue and pity why I was there.

The receptionist passed me a health history form. As I sat with the clipboard in my lap filling it out I was surprised to think back over my family history and put down the dates that my grandmother, mother, and sister had been diagnosed with their breast cancers. It felt like a lot of information to squeeze into the small line they provided on the form.

The technician that came to take me to my exam looked like Chrissy from *Three's Company*, but with big, New Jersey hair.

She handed me a robe and left the room while I got changed. Coming back in the room a few minutes later she rubbed her hands together, apologizing for her cold hands and then went right ahead and laid those icy things on my breasts. Pulling me over to the mammography machine they were flattened, kneaded and pulled like pizza dough while the lab tech tried to line them up on the mammography baking sheet.

After taking each image she would return to do a little more kneading and then excuse herself from the toxic rays being shot at my chest. It felt completely ironic to be undergoing something so potentially dangerous to the very breasts I was trying to protect, but this was the protocol. Six images later, "Chrissy" told me to put my clothes back on and wait in the room. She returned after only a few moments and looked down at the floor as she told me I should return to the waiting room until I was called again.

I walked down the hallway and felt like I was in an Alice in Wonderland world. The corridor got narrower the farther I walked. My brain was in a panic, shooting off thoughts and questions. Was this the routine procedure? Shouldn't she be telling me that someone would call with the results in a few weeks? What was I waiting for? What did they see on my films?

The next technician who came to get me had a better disposition from the start.

"Ms. Koo-bee," she said, "I'm ready to take you back."

"Thanks," I said, standing up, "It's Cub-bee, like where you put your stuff when you were in preschool."

"Oh cute. Follow me sweetheart," she said and ushered me toward a different part of the building. As she walked down the hall, she scanned my chart. "You're so young," she said, making a little tutting noise that make me feel like she was in solidarity with my thinking that I shouldn't be there.

Once we were in the exam room she said, "The radiologist suggested we do an ultrasound of your breasts."

"Is that normal?" I asked, really hoping she would say it was.

"Your breasts are very dense due to your age so it is hard to get a good picture."

My thoughts were stuck back at her use of the word "we." I felt far from connected to this random person in a lab coat and this breast-imaging center in the middle of a state that was 3,000 miles from my home.

As she covered my breast in cold jelly, I began to weep. I had always imagined my first ultrasound would be with Mitchel standing next to me, holding my hand, our eyes fixed with anticipation on the screen waiting to view the life inside my body for the first time. This was far from that experience. This was the search for looming death, not new life.

CHAPTER 8

DOOZIES

The first few days after my mammogram I conjured up all the worst-case scenarios I could imagine. This preoccupation with dire outcomes in the days after a test or screening would become a most dreaded ritual in my life over the next few years. Then the news I feared arrived in a business sized envelope. Inside was a single sheet of paper, with a letterhead followed by this: "Image of left breast quadrant finds a hypo echoic solid oval shaped density measuring 14x7x15mm."

I tried to continue to read but the words were fuzzy through my tears. I went to the phone and called Mitchel at school. Luckily he wasn't in class, so he answered and assured me it was nothing. He tried, but I could hear the stress in his voice. This expression, of support and love, mixed with fear and sadness was one I would come to know very well. I was blessed that he would become my husband.

I decided to wait until after our wedding to do the biopsy, finding a place in my mind to compartmentalize the news for a while. The stress of not knowing what the oval shaped density might be seemed easier to handle than the possibility that I might find out I had cancer and have to carry this information with me down the aisle. I didn't want breast cancer in my wedding photos, and it was not the dowry I hoped to offer my husband.

Two months later, after the glow of our wedding and honeymoon had faded, I embarked on my next "rite of passage event," my first surgery. It was my first time in life under general anesthesia. I had no idea what to expect, which, thankfully, helped me from getting too scared. I did feel young to be dealing with any of this.

Leaving my biopsy in my post-surgery drugged out daze, I looked out the window of our car to a wet April day in New Jersey. Our Honda was a bit dirty, so everything looked a bit smudgy through the window. Across the street on the grass was a long sign near the entrance to a parking lot—New Jersey Cancer Center. I zipped my fleece up higher, closed my eyes and made a wish that I wouldn't be getting to know that place.

Two weeks later, when life had done what it does, and returned back to a relative normal, we got the best wedding gift of all. This one came in a business-sized envelope from the doctor who performed the biopsy; a negative result stating that my lump was only scarred muscle tissue, and nothing to be concerned about.

As a celebration of my health, the resiliency of my mom and sister, and in memory of my mother-in-law Marcia who also had breast cancer, Mitchel and I signed up for the Avon Breast Cancer 3-Day. We would walk three days, about 20 miles each day, from Bear Mountain in upstate New York to Central Park in downtown Manhattan. This was an amazing event, with stellar participants, a rocking staff, all for an important and unifying cause.

The opening ceremonies started early on a Friday morning in late August. Fog rolled off the lawns of the park as the throngs of participants got psyched for the adventure before them. Music boomed from huge speakers at every corner of the large grass welcoming area. The stage was full of inspirational speakers sharing stories and memories and a sea of every shade of pink imaginable surrounded me. I could see the back of the head of a guy a few lines of people ahead. His scalp was shaved clean leaving only a ribbon-shaped patch of hair at the back that he had dyed pink. He stood hand in hand with his wife, also bald, wearing a pink cap that stated, "Cancer Sucks." In that man, I saw someone who would stick by his wife through thick and thin. As I looked over at Mitchel, I knew that we too were those kinds of people, though I hoped we wouldn't have to endure cancer ourselves.

Walking that first day we bounced along the route, slowing down to talk with people and hear and exchange stories. We met three women from Westchester who were doing the walk in honor of a fourth friend with breast cancer who couldn't be there. Every conversation thereafter was equally as inspiring. People walking for their teachers, their cousin, and their best friends, as well as their mothers. So many of them were already survivors. I felt alive and energized to be part of this community. Full of the adrenaline of the event, the miles passed quickly.

About halfway through the second day, however, stories about how badly everyone slept in the overcrowded tents seemed more prevalent than stories of strength and survival. By the end of that day and 43 miles total behind us, our feet were sore and covered in moleskin. We were tired, a bit less excited about another night of sleeping on the ground, and a tad bit wondering why we had decided to do this.

But then we were reminded.

Mitchel and I were washing up before retiring to our tent. Streams of the 3-Day staffers with their neon green t-shirts started running all over camp telling people to come out to the day's finish-line to cheer on a participant who was just completing the miles. When we got to a spot along the last 500 feet of the road to the finish, a woman slowly and steadily came toward us, hobbling her way leaning on one crutch. It had been more than two hours since Mitchel and I had come into camp. As she got closer I could see how young she was, probably close to my age. She was wearing a survivor version of the 3-Day shirt reserved for those who had battled the disease. While she looked incredibly tired, she also looked like an image of strength. Her head held high, taking each step without slowing down. She personified the survivor: determined, strong and courageous.

I have had moments in life wondering if cancer hits those who can handle it most. This seemed true for the woman hobbling to the finish of the 3-Day, and I knew it to be the case for my mom and sister. Neither of them ever complained about their illness, pain, or discomfort. And never once did they look like cancer was going to defeat them.

CHAPTER 9

FEMALE FAMILY JEWELS

The millennium was off to a good start. Life was finding a nice flow, graduate school was stimulating, Mitchel loved his program, married life was lovely, and New Jersey was turning out to be better than I had imagined it would be. Lisa and Mom were now solidly survivors and breast cancer slowly moved to the background of our lives.

Until the end of the year 2000.

Just like the first tumor, Lisa found a second one in her other breast, when she was in the shower. Unlike the first time, Lisa knew it was cancer as soon as she touched it, and it was confirmed a week later.

Just after New Years, Lisa underwent her second mastectomy and reconstruction. But one thing was different on this go-round. It had been eight years since Lisa's first breast cancer and during that time, research had identified two genetic mutations, BRCA 1 and 2, which put individuals at high risk for early onset breast and ovarian cancer, and the gene was most common in people of Ashkenazi Jewish decent, our family's ancestry. Due to her multiple occurrences of breast cancer, the first at the young age of 36, she was urged to undergo genetic testing.

Lisa was tested and got a positive result for the BRCA2 genetic mutation.

While there was really nothing Lisa could do regarding her breast tissue after two complete mastectomies, there were some issues and options she might still want to consider were she to get a positive test result. One new treatment being used in high-risk cases was chemoprevention, where natural, synthetic or biologic substances were used to reverse, suppress or prevent cancer. Additionally, those who tested positively for the gene could decrease their risk for breast cancer and ovarian cancer substantially by undergoing the removal of their ovaries and fallopian tubes. The other argument for testing which resonated with Lisa was to be a part of helping move along the process of finding a cure for this disease by being part of the research.

My mom was devastated. Though it wasn't clear whether she or Pop was the carrier, my mom assumed she had passed this along, or took responsibility for it whether or not she was the driving force. Clearly this was not the legacy she intended to pass along, and her guilt about it was obvious.

While the information was redeeming in that it shed new light on how Lisa might move forward with her cancer treatment, it was not a preemptive approach. The stakes were different however when it came to me. Lisa's diagnosis of being BRCA2 positive meant that I also had a 50 percent chance of carrying the genetic mutation. In my case, the information could be used before getting cancer in much greater ways. Knowing this information would provide increased opportunities for surveillance, chemoprevention or surgery, and decrease my chances of becoming a "survivor."

Knowledge of her genetic status did give Lisa a fight she was ready to wage. Since there was little Lisa could do now to help herself, she felt it was her duty to help me, help myself. Lisa was trying to protect me like only a loving sister would. So began her campaign to get me tested.

The first time Lisa talked to me about the test was a few months after her second diagnosis when Mitchel and I met up with her and my mom in Florida for a winter get-away. My mom had planned the trip as part of a graduation gift for me and a recovery gift for my sister. Over coffee and cottage cheese one morning in the rattan-furnished breakfast nook of our rented condo, Lisa told me about her genetic status and how it would affect me. It didn't even faze me. I was stuck in New Jersey, far from my family and friends and just starting to decode who I was. My focus was on graduate school and the only question about my future at that moment was what I would do with my Masters of Public Health once I graduated. I didn't have kids yet and had only a small semblance of an idea of where "home" would eventually be.

The furthest thing from my mind was whether or not I carried some crazy gene that could give me cancer.

CHAPTER 10

FRIED EGGS

It was a big moment, Match Day, where thousands of graduate students in Psychology gathered around their computers, and at one moment, found out where they would be living and working for the next year. Mitchel and I were hovered around our small desktop computer in the nook, the name we gave the narrow office space in our apartment. Mitchel hit refresh on the computer right at 8 am when the list went live. He was nervous, hands shaking as he typed in his unique key code and waited for the system to recognize him. Suddenly the sentence we hoped for flashed across the screen. "Mitchel G. Adler, you have matched to your first choice, UC Davis." Before I had a chance to read further we were hugging and jumping up and down as we held each other. Mitchel was making due on his promise to bring me back to California. We were coming home.

It was a few minutes after five in the morning on the West Coast when I called my mom to share the great news, so I was surprised when Pop answered the phone. I wasn't expecting him to be at my mom's place in Menlo Park in the first place. He had come from San Luis Obispo the previous week to take her to some doctors' appointments, but I thought he would be back by now. I had planned to call him after my mom.

His voice sounded a bit concerned at first, but I figured he wasn't expecting the phone to ring at that hour. He called down the hallway to my mom's bedroom, "Dod, pick up the phone, Hun. Raychel's on the line."

My heart was beating like hummingbird wings with the excitement of telling them our news. I could hear my dad's breathing on the phone, but rather than make small talk I waited out the awkward quiet until my mom was on the other line.

I wasn't in any way prepared for the buzz kill of how the conversation went.

My mom had news of her own. She and Pop had just visited several doctors to try to identify why her cold and cough wouldn't go away. A chest x-ray revealed a large, inoperable mass on her lung and she was being staged for lung cancer.

Suddenly my homecoming took on even greater meaning.

As we packed up our lives in New Jersey, and closed four years on the east coast, my heart was heavy, not the way I had imagined I would feel about getting back to California, and my family and friends there. For years I had been waiting for this moment to get back to California, but now there was sadness and dread. Hiding out in New Jersey so I didn't have to face my mom's illness seemed like a fine option.

Maybe New Jersey wasn't so bad after all. It had shown me that there are good people wherever you go, I now understood the majestic colors of fall in the Northeast, and I had learned how to drive in the snow. I had come to enjoy real bagels, not bread in a circle, and delis and kosher pickles, and of course pizza, with crusts so thin you needed to lift the plate to your mouth to take a bite. I had built a deeper relationship with Mitchel's father and sister than I could ever have made on short trips and vacations. And, although Lisa and the boys had still been a five-hour trip away from our home in New Jersey, somehow being able to travel by car or train instead of a plane made them seem much closer.

These things and more I would miss.

Our homecoming was bittersweet. It was lovely to be able to spend time with old friends, and equally wonderful to be meeting new folks and experiencing a new place. Mitchel and I were enjoying our jobs and our first time with both of us making large enough paychecks to have some money to burn.

But it was hard to make friends and feel settled when we were making the two-hour drive to Palo Alto each weekend, and Mom's demise was coming quickly. I had never seen her sick a single day as a child, and now she was in and out of the hospital, and losing abilities we had both taken for granted all our lives.

My mom only made it to Davis twice. The first time was in September, right after we'd moved back, and on that trip, Mom had no problem walking through the rooms, commenting on the carpet and the bright yellow, green, and blue colors we had painted. I could tell she was so happy to have us back in California and be at our house.

By her next visit for Thanksgiving, she was confined to a wheelchair and the carpets that covered our apartment made her alert to how quickly she was declining. With her life of tennis, dance and water aerobics no longer a reality, my mom became keenly aware of her impending departure from the earth. Visibly depressed by her situation, and not talking much, she seemed like an empty alter ego of herself—not her full of hope and peppy ways.

My pop, brother, sister, and nephews had all come together at our house to celebrate the day of giving thanks and what was bound to be my mom's last birthday.

Unfortunately, our apartment, almost entirely covered in carpet was not an easy place for her to maneuver the wheelchair, so she stayed in the first spot in our living room where my father had docked her, her bottom lip jutted out in disappointment.

As this was my first time hosting my family for Thanksgiving, I prepared an elaborate vegetarian feast which called for an insane amount of potatoes, carrots and hard skinned squash.

Spending most of the morning in our small kitchen peeling and chopping, I didn't get much chance to interact with my mom. I was busy creating a Thanksgiving dinner heavy on the sides and salad to hide the fact that there was no turkey. But by noon, the Tofurkey that I hoped to pull off as the real deal was the least of my worries. The sink was clogged before I was done prepping the meal. I had overworked the garbage disposal with all the peels.

"The disposal's toast," I said, calling out to everyone in the living room, who were pretending to watch a football game so they didn't have to acknowledge the pain of the occasion.

But the bubble of denial popped when my mom, never having heard that expression before, thought it was the perfect way to describe her condition and spent the rest of the evening and all through our meal declaring, "I'm toast!" It was simultaneously mortifying to hear her declaring herself done and uncomfortably comical. Pop and Joel took advantage of an opportunity to remove themselves from the situation by offering to wash the first round of dishes in buckets outside on our postage stamp sized yard.

When I think back on that day, I feel guilty that my mom's last Thanksgiving was with a fake turkey.

CHAPTER 11

DOUBLE WHAMMIES

As terrible as it sounded, and as much as I didn't want to hear it, my mom was nearing the end. It was clear she was not going to turn back and have a new lease on life. It was so clear that two weeks later I learned about the words "palliative care." My mom had reached a final life stage that many know as Hospice. This organization and its wonderful people and resources come in to ease the transition from life to death for both the patient and their loved ones.

Hospice Care workers were around the house daily during the week, helping bathe my mom, set up her pill box, and do some light cleaning around the house. On weekends Mitchel and I would come down to help Pop, who have moved back in to help care for her.

One weekend toward the end of February I was with my mom and our eyes caught each other and held together frozen as we shared a look realizing that she was about to die. She had been bed bound for a few weeks at that point, occasionally getting up with assistance to go to the living room for a little TV or change of scenery or to the dining table where she ate, first only chocolate shakes from her favorite local burger joint, then yogurts, and then nothing.

She was in bed and I was sitting on the edge of it, playing Gin Rummy with her. After a few turns had passed between us, I looked up at Mom's cards and saw she was holding many more than the requisite ten. I must not have shown my poker face, because she noticed the look of concern on my face. My mom had been the one who taught me how to play every card game I knew. And she made sure to teach me all the right moves and strategies as well—like how to count cards, watch for tricks, and never give away your hand. Mom gave me a sad, knowing face that said, "I just don't have it anymore."

Though this first look into the face of death was difficult, the hardest day was four weeks later. When I visited, my mom, who had thrown me homemade birthday parties the first 18 years of my life, didn't even realize it was March 30th, my 30th birthday. It was a strange and painful way to bring in the next decade knowing it would be without my mom, realizing that she would not know the children I hoped to have, or see where my adult life would take me.

Pop tried to make a celebration. He bought a tiny chocolate cake from the Safeway bakery and put on a cheery face while my mom stayed in her bedroom down the hall unaware of our melancholy fete.

Most of the conversations I had with my mom in those final weeks left me feeling disconnected and confused. I didn't know how to respond when she called out for her estranged brother Mickey, who hadn't spoken to her for 35 years. I thought it was the morphine clouding her mind and asked the Hospice nurse if there was a way to decrease the dosage just enough that she wouldn't have pain, but so that we could have some meaningful conversations. I wanted to hold on to the last moments I could have with my mom and didn't want our time to be filled with nonsensical outbursts that just left me frustrated and sad. The hospice nurse suggested I look at a book called "Final Gifts" and offered to bring me a copy on her next home care visit.

The next day I read the entire thing cover to cover while my mom napped. Suddenly all the things my mom had been saying and doing that seemed crazy to me were given meaning and a title, "Nearing Death Awareness." The book posits that as a person gets closer to death, they will use language that is often symbolic and can seem to be nonsensical but is really the dying patient's way of making sense of death, closing up loose ends, or sharing last wishes.

Later that afternoon, I was sitting next to my mom on her bed and she asked me who the girl with green hair was sitting next to me. Having just finished reading "Final Gifts," I was prepped for how to engage her and steer the conversation instead of just giving up or getting frustrated by her questions.

I tried to think deeply about what the green hair could represent and who the girl was. The only thing I could figure was that, as a kid my hair had always been green from chlorine during the summer swim season.

"Yes, Mom, remember how green my hair used to get with all that swimming? We never knew how to get it out, did we?" I tried to bring comfort to the conversation by reminiscing about a sweet memory from our past.

"No, not you, the little one sitting next to you. Why did she come here?" she asked, seemingly more curious about the girl than concerned.

"I'm not sure, Mom," I said, and then remembering what I'd read about reassuring the loved one I added, "I guess she really wants to be sure you are okay and comfortable."

"Do you know her?" she asked me. "It seems that she knows you, but I can't tell if she knows who I am."

The hairs on my arm stood on end.

A few weeks before, when she was still able to get to the dining room table, my mom asked Mitchel and me if we intended to have children soon.

"We hope so," I said, holding back my tears, the pain of acknowledging that she would not meet our children obvious to us all.

"I will see them," she said, "and you. I will be watching and loving you, I promise."

Perhaps the girl with the green hair was my unborn child and had come to meet my mom before she left the earth. I would have a girl. She was letting me know this, and comforting me by sharing that she was aware of the child I would conceive.

A week later on my next visit, the dreamy conversations stopped and my mom's day was filled with sleep, her eyes closed more than open. Occasionally she would open them slightly, her eyeballs rolling about and her emaciated arms just barely lifting from the bed gesturing awkwardly, pointing her finger off toward the corner of the room. That day I decided it was time to tell Mom that she could go, that I would be okay, we all would.

The next week Pop called us on Friday morning and suggested that we come before the weekend. Joel was on his way from Santa Cruz, and my dad had bought Lisa a ticket on a flight that was leaving Rochester later that day.

"It doesn't seem like she's going to make it much longer," Pop said. "The Hospice nurse today said her breath had changed and was slowing down."

I had read all about this in the hospice book. The end was near.

By the time Mitchel and I got down to my mom's place, my dad had already assembled a few important people to say their good-byes. Our close family friend, Antonia Tu, was there, as well as two of my mom's tennis buddies. Later in the afternoon my mom's favorite Rabbi, Janet Marder, came to say good-bye, and we sang some *niggunim*, religious songs that are a form of vocal instrumental music, often without lyrics. These were meant to soothe my mom and offer her healing and comfort.

I was afraid to leave her that night so I set up a sleeping bag next to her bed and drifted off for a few hours. By morning, Pop reported the changes to my mom's skin and temperature by phone to the hospice nurse. She asked Pop if there was anyone else we were waiting on for good-byes. He let her know that those of us in the local area were here, but that Lisa and Joel wouldn't be flying in until the next day. The hospice nurse said she didn't think my mom could hold out much longer. Then she gave Pop detailed instruction in how to administer morphine to my mom over the next few hours.

I went to shower and change and by the time I came back to my mom's room, Pop had transformed the space from sickly to inspiring. He had opened the sliding glass doors in my mom's room that opened to her third floor penthouse patio. All the medication bottles and medical equipment that previously filled her bedside tables had been moved into the bathroom. Vases of flowers and photos filled the space instead. Pop had carried in chairs from the living room and encircled the bed with them, giving us each a place to participate in this final act of my mother's life. He sat on the chair closest to her head, holding her hand in his. I could tell from the tears on his cheeks that he had been saying his good-bye to her. Though they had spent the past few years living apart, my parents had remained dear and loving friends always. He was struggling to let go.

Mitchel and I came and joined Pop around the bed, and Pop suggested we each take a moment to say what we wanted to say to her privately. Anton went in first, then Mitchel, and then it was time for me to have my final moments alone with her. I could think of no other way to say good-bye to my mom than to thank her for all the love and caring she had given me all my life. I told her that I would miss her terribly, but that I would be okay.

When we all returned together to her bedside, Pop put in one of my mom's Barbra Streisand CDs into the stereo he had brought into the room. The sweeping emotions of the music were the perfect background, my mom's soundtrack of dying. As the last song came on, my mom's breath began to change. Short little gasps and then an exhale and a few seconds where it seemed she had stopped breathing before the cycle started again. And then, an orchestration so perfect it didn't seem possible, my mother's breaths began to slow, and as the music stopped, so did her life.

But life works in mysterious ways sometimes. One week after my mom died, I missed my period and took a pregnancy test. The pink plus sign in the window suggested maybe my mom really had seen a little girl with green hair, a vision of my child to be.

Five weeks later, I was at home feeling crampy and nauseous, so I got into bed. A few minutes later I felt wetness between my legs, like the feeling of sitting on a wet bike seat where even my pants felt damp. When I pulled back the covers, I could see the stain of blood on my sheet. We called the Advice Nurse at the hospital put into words what we feared—"You've suffered a miscarriage."

In the midst of mourning came more mourning. My mom, and my first fertilized egg, gone.

CHAPTER 12

JUGS

Mourning my mom and my miscarriage was a challenging pairing. It was enough just being sad that my mom was gone, but to also feel I had lost the baby my mom had "seen" right before she died seemed completely unfair.

Yet while my sadness at these losses was deep, my emotions were confused by the drive I felt to become a mom. Somehow my longing to fill the void of being mothered transferred into an even stronger desire to be a mother. Supporting my wishes to move forward with building our family, Mitchel and I got busy with that special brand of conception sex that is completely calculated to the internal temperatures and moistness of the lady partner, while trying to add in a bit of spontaneity and spice wherever we could. Five weeks later, the second pregnancy test in the box of two I had purchased at Costco confirmed we were pregnant again.

It wasn't much longer until I busted out with my first set of pregnancy boobs. They were like teenagers experiencing an early rush of love: hot, heavy, and ready to rock. My friend Heidi was the first person to point them out. We were meeting up in the Mission District in San Francisco to go dancing for our friend's birthday. I barely stepped out of the car and onto the curb when Heidi blurted out, "You're looking busty, girl!" with a smile on her face that told me she knew why. Sure enough, a third bulge began to grow below my breasts over the next nine months. Pregnancy boobs are the best—full, warm, and plump with new life.

Soon they were bursting with milk and ready to provide for their newest fan, Marleyna, my baby girl. Her name was a mash-up of Mitchel's mom, Marcia, and my mom, Elena. From the start we called her Marley, and born on Valentine's Day, she was a little package of love.

Unfortunately nursing didn't come quite as naturally as it did on the pre-natal video we watched during our birthing class. The video baby just wriggled on up to its mama's bosom and started sucking away. Marley would make her way up to my breast, but just couldn't seem to get the right grab. June, the lactation consultant at Sutter Davis Hospital shared all her ideas and tips including a little song we could sing to encourage Marley to open her mouth wide enough to nurse. "Oooopen," I would sing in a high lilting voice, as I gently rubbed between her mouth and chin encouraging her mouth to open to its biggest circumference.

I wasn't well warned about all the pains of nursing. It all seemed so natural, loving, and wonderful in the books and images I had seen beforehand. But nursing with Marley posed some challenges. Those first few months I endured cracked and bloody nipples, several instances of mastitis (clogged milk ducts), and the occasional bite on the booby by some very sharp, freshly cut teeth. But I believed that nursing my newborn was one of the most important jobs I had, so I persisted.

And then we hit the jackpot and I became a milk machine, the Kubby Adler Organic Dairy. My humps became the "dynamic duo," cranking away to provide all day and into wee hours of the night.

I was whipping out my breasts all the time and pretty much everywhere. Most of the time I didn't even bother putting on a bra, but if I did try to gussy up that day, the snaps at the front of my nursing bra would be hastily pulled into place but not fastened. It wasn't worth the effort since the routine would invariably begin again in just an hour or less. Nurse, burp, clean diaper, sleep, a little "playtime," and repeat. Going into pregnancy I had been duly warned of how "me" time would give way to full time baby time, but I didn't quite realize how much of that would be spent nursing. After just two weeks there was an indentation in our couch from where I spent most of the day nursing, with short reading breaks in between.

The first few days home from the hospital Pop would bring me a blanket to cover myself when he saw me getting into position to nurse on the couch. He even suggested I go into another room when our family friend, Anton, came to meet the baby. But his modesty was way beyond mine. I tried a few times to use a cover-up, which I had seen more elegant moms pull off very well, but it didn't work for me. I spent the whole time wrangling the nursing cover, loosening Marley's grasp and then fully exposing myself at the moment of most audaciousness as I squeezed my breast and plowed Marley's mouth into my mound to get her latched on in position.

Even with all the down time on the couch, just me, Marley and my boobs, three months passed too quickly, and no sooner had I gotten the hang of my new baby, than my maternity *leave* was over and I became a mother, *leaving*. The night before my return to work, I hosted book club at my house and spent the entire evening crying my eyes out about leaving my precious little bundle to give my time and energy to strangers. I was the only one in the group that was working at the time, and while they consoled me and told me Marley would be fine, I worried deep down that they all were thinking that I was traumatizing my baby and was already being dubbed a "bad mom."

But come sunrise, I put on my work clothes, a bit snugger than before being pregnant, slipped some breast pads into my bra to prevent leakage from staining my shirt, and returned part-time to the workforce at the California State Department of Health.

While I was busy being a worker bee, Marley went to a small family day care in our neighborhood.

In order to leave the childcare provider with milk rather than formula, I needed to pump throughout the day to keep up my supply, so I made a new "breast" friend, the Medela Pump in Style Original Breast Pump. Whenever my breasts would start to ache or I could feel a bit of moisture collecting on my breast pads, I would excuse myself from what I was doing and head for the basement of our building that housed the "Mother's Room."

Lucky for me that a California law had passed two years earlier mandating that every employer provide a "reasonable amount of time" to express breast milk as well as make "reasonable efforts" to give these lactating women a place to do so in private. My work place was doing okay on the first part of the legislation, though it could hardly pass for reasonable in terms of the space.

For our entire building of close to 1,000 employees we had three breast-feeding stalls, divided by thin blue, hospital-grade curtains. In each stall was a chair, and attached to the back wall, a four-inch wide flat surface that could barely hold the breast pump.

The other challenge was that the lights in the room, following another California code for energy efficiency in new buildings, were set on a motion sensor, which often meant that the lights went out after ten minutes of pumping, because I could barely move or else the pump would fall off the narrow counter. There I would sit in the dark; my breasts chained to the pump, trying to gesture wildly with my arms so that I would trigger the sensor and turn the lights back on.

The heating and air systems also caused nuisances as the air didn't seem to reach the basement of the building. In the summer, when I had just returned from my leave and was new to pumping, I could barely keep my sweaty cleavage from sliding out of the nipple shield centered on my breasts. By winter, I was a pro, but my nipples were frozen into the cups.

Despite these obstacles, the worst scenario was when another lactating woman was in the room at the same time, as I found it difficult to inspire milk production with the sounds of another machine sucking at the nipples of the woman in the next stall. I felt like a dairy cow strapped to a milking machine, it was "udderly" impossible to get comfortable. My best chance of some pittance of milk was to bring a super cute picture of Marley to look at while I pumped, and pray that the other nursing women in the building were out to lunch.

All in all though, I felt like I had a handle on being a working mom, both in and out of the office. I had a beautiful and healthy baby, nursing was bringing back my figure, my work and family life were rewarding, and across the country, Lisa was doing well, and my mom was surely beaming down on all of us with a huge smile on her face.

CHAPTER 13

BOOBY MOUNTAINS

Taking on the role of being a mother, in the absence of my mom's guidance and assistance with the new rituals and experiences of motherhood, was devastating. Not that my mom would have really been the doting grandmother of my dreams—she would have been all about buying the outfits, but then would want the baby to sit and not fuss, while she went on to her day's activities. The irony of the situation was that Lisa was actually much more capable and fluent in the kind of mothering I wanted to practice, more than my mom would ever have been. Still, the experience of having your child nurtured by the person who nurtured you was something I missed. Lisa understood this and worked hard to make sure that my transition into motherhood was as smooth as possible by being a part of many of the key "firsts."

For all our lives, Lisa and I had been switching off the role of big or little sister depending on our needs at the time. Of course, in my early years, Lisa was clearly in the big sister role due to her age and abilities, but over the years I stepped into the role of seniority and supported her.

At my wedding party, Lisa said to the guests in her Matron-Of-Honor speech, "I know Raychel will deny this, but although she's my little sister, she's always been much wiser and more mature."

I thanked Lisa for her thoughtful words and then denied them just as she said I would. But I agree that there was *some* truth to what she shared. Somewhere along our relationship Lisa had put me on a pedestal, believing that I held more advanced emotional intelligence than she possessed. In her opinion, I handled things better, and with less stress and anxiety. She felt that she had paved the way for me with Pop by being the bad girl and leaving nothing more terrible for me to do to wrong him. She saw me as more successful in my solid marriage, savvier with finances, better with words, and calmer in the face of authority. Due to this, Lisa respected my advice, and would seek it often. I, on the other hand, shared all my hopes and fears, concerns and questions with her because she was my best friend and confidant, and I was looking more for support and solidarity than answers.

It was a thrill for Lisa and me to have the chance to be mothers together and to have our children know each other. We dubbed ourselves "sister mothers," a special time in our relationship when we raised our children together.

The best thrill was watching our children play with each other. I could sit enthralled for hours watching Dylan and Elliott hold Marley and gently toss her in the air as I had done with them when they were babies.

We were a strange configuration of generations for such close relations. Cousins 13 years apart, an aunt only 17 years older than her nephew, and two moms who are sisters separated by 16 years. Asymmetric, but full of love.

Those early years getting to know myself as a mom, Marley as my child and the new realms of family with Mitchel are some of the sweetest and relatively carefree times I can remember. Lisa was doing well health-wise and, during those first few years of Marley's life, we committed to staying connected. We talked frequently on the phone, sent each other emails on a regular basis, and traveled to see each other as much as was possible with my small kid in tow.

There were a good two years of these relatively calm waters, a focus on new life rather than on sickness and dying. We were a young family, a threesome enjoying the freshness of babyhood and parenting.

But just as Mitchel and I were about to announce that Baby Number Two was on her way, there was other news that would pop our baby bliss bubble.

"Have you talked with Lisa?" Pop asked. We had just arrived at his condo in Menlo Park and were unfastening Marley from her car seat carrier when he dropped the bomb. I knew full well from the other times that nothing good was going to follow that question.

"No," I said, "What's up with her?" My face started to cringe in anticipation.

"Her cancer is back. It's metastasized to the bone in her spine. You should call her."

"Of course," I said, and walked into the kitchen, picked up the phone, and punched Lisa's number into the keypad in a zombie-like movement of just moving forward because that is the only thing I could figure to do.

"Lis, its Raych."

"Hi, Ray Ray," Lisa said. Her voice sounded like she expected my call. "I guess Pop told you my news." I could hear her sadness, but she also sounded more grounded than I imagined she would be.

"Yeah, he did. I'm so sorry, Lis. Ugg, this totally sucks. I'm so sorry." My brain was numb and I couldn't think of anything more intelligent to say so I stopped.

"I know, it does, but, what can you do?"

"You can fight it is what you can do. And I know you will. You're a trooper, always have been." I felt like a cheerleader trying to rouse the crowd of a losing team, but I knew it was what she needed to hear.

"I'll call you next week after my appointment with the oncologist. I should have a better sense of what the protocol will be for dealing with this after I talk with him."

I hung up the phone and Mitchel was there to hold me tight. He knew I had held back and understood without speaking that I didn't want to shift the focus away from what Lisa was dealing with to share my own news. I decided not to tell Pop that weekend either. Somehow withholding the information that I was pregnant again seemed to allow a sacred space for both Lisa's illness and my pregnancy.

Over the next months, Lisa was busy making trips to the oncologist, getting radiation to her spine, which sapped the life from her body. Meanwhile, I was making monthly trips to the Ob/ Gyn and midwife, having ultrasounds, and building a life inside my body.

CHAPTER 14

MILK SHAKES

Lisa had ulterior motives for this trip. She couched her personal agenda inside the guise of getting me ready for the birth of my next daughter, but I could see through her thinly veiled plans. While she had brought up the genetic testing conversation every now and again over the years, I was more poised to take action on her words at this point in my life. My second daughter was on her way soon, and we were not planning to have any more children, so soon enough my nursing breasts would be through with their work. Plus the progression of Lisa's disease added urgency to her plea. This represented a terminal phase of a disease she had lived with for years, and it wouldn't be long. For both of us, the ante had been upped.

"This is such a chance for you, Ray Ray," Lisa said, barely sitting in her chair as she leaned across the table, the closeness of her face lending urgency to her pleading.

"You can have a different reality," she continued. "You don't have to be wondering when you're going to die."

The word "die" made me bristle. Although we both knew that death wasn't far away for her, saying it out loud made it more real.

I had always assumed I was a carbon copy of my sister Lisa. It seemed we were passed the same genetic code. Thinking about her dying was like imagining a piece of me dying as well.

"Lis, I totally get where you're coming from, but look at me. I have one little girl in there," I said, pointing to my daughter Marley's room down the hall, "and another one in here," I said as I gestured at my belly. "I have to breast feed and be a mommy right now, not think about cutting off my breasts."

"Just get tested," she said. "You don't have to do anything right now, but at least you'll know." I could tell Lisa was not letting down this time.

Lisa was right that I didn't have to do anything after being tested, but I knew if I found out I had the gene, I wouldn't be able to just sit around and not address the information. A positive result would be like blowing air on a raging fire, making it grow bigger and burn faster. I wanted to stay in my little cocoon of not knowing for a little while longer. I wanted to savor the sweetness of nursing my last child and enjoy days of being a young mom with only the cares of a newborn weighing on me.

At the same time I realized how important it was for Lisa to know that her legacy would live on by my being tested. I wanted her to know that.

I looked across the room at Lisa, her warm ocean blue eyes reaching deeply into mine. The left side of her face drooped down in an expression I had seen before when she was tired or stressed. It looked almost as if she had a stroke; her tears and fears were morphing her profile. How many times had I looked at Lisa's life as a map of my future—seeing in her what lay ahead for me. Yet at that moment I noticed something new. Her face did not look like a mirrored reflection of mine, but more like a face reflected through water, rippled and constantly shifting.

I looked at my sister and for the first time I could see how we were different—not carbon copies but rather asymmetrical versions of the same material. The choices I had made this far in my life were my own. Her influence was undeniable: the paths crossed, but they were unique.

"I will get tested, Lis. I can promise us both that. I just want to wait until I'm ready to make choices based on what I find out, or don't."

Earlier that day Lisa and I had been on a walk in Menlo Park while visiting Pop. Dylan and Elliott were walking ahead with Mitchel, while Lisa and I were having fun trying to come up with potential names for the baby in my belly. Lisa had a penchant for pop icon names. She had named Dylan after Bob Dylan and Dylan Thomas, and Elliott after the little boy's character in the movie E.T." How about Ruby? Like in the Stones tune *'Ruby Tuesday'*?" Lisa asked.

"I like the ring of Ruby," I said.

"You know, Mom's mother Naomi, her maiden name was Rubin," Lisa said.

"And her dad's first name was Rufus," I added.

It seemed that maybe Lisa was on to something with this name and its connection to our family. I had been struggling with how to follow the Jewish tradition that a baby be named after a deceased relative. Since Marley's full name, Marleyna was derived by combining the name of Mitchel's mother Marcia, and that of my mom, Elena. There were, thankfully, no other immediate relatives to name after. Mitchel had a deceased grandfather, Russell, so the "r-u" of Ruby's name had meaning on both sides of our family.

"It's my birthstone too, rubies for July," Lisa said. I thought about how sadly ironic it was that Lisa's astrological sign was Cancer. She had been marked from the beginning.

A knot grew in my throat as I realized that Lisa would probably not live past the baby girl's first few birthdays. I would name this child for my sister. Ruby sounded like someone who could give a big full-bellied laugh and would look at the world in front of her with a lot of wonder and excitement. She would fit right in with the female lineage of our family.

During that walk I realized that while I had focused so much on my personal experience with genetic testing, I hadn't stopped to consider that I was passing along this fate to this little girl, and to Marley, too. Feelings of dread and guilt caught in my heart. Lisa had given birth to sons, who, though not genetically immune to their mother's breast cancer, were in a much safer demographic than my daughters would be.

When I snapped out of the thoughts of our walk earlier that day I was brought back to the kitchen and my choice was suddenly clear.

"It's a gift, Lis, what you are doing for me," I said to her. "I wish that you didn't have it to give to me, but I appreciate it none-the-less. It'll be different for me. Different in good ways."

CHAPTER 15

POINTER SISTERS

You can tell a lot about a relationship based on who you would want with you at pivotal times in life—giving birth probably suggesting the most intimate of relationships. Without my mom in play, and not wanting Pop or Joel in the delivery room with me, along with Mitchel, and our midwife Amie, Lisa is the one and only extra person I felt I could give birth in front of. Lisa and I took a gamble on when I would deliver. I had been almost two weeks late with Marley, but this was my second birth which tend to come earlier—so we went for six days past due date and bought tickets for Lisa to come out and either be with me in the birthing room, or shortly thereafter.

I didn't realize immediately when my water broke. I recall the sound of a pop at one point when I was sitting at the table trying to put on my tennis shoes, but I didn't feel the gush of water until I stood up to put the leash on Monty, our black lab. With Marley my water bag never broke. They broke it for me when we arrived at the hospital. So, this was a new feeling. I gave an apologetic look to the dog that was now not going on a walk, got my phone from my bag and called Mitchel. Lisa was the second call I made.

"You were right," I said to Lisa as soon as she picked up. "April 8th. I'm giving birth five days late. I'm sad that you won't get here in time, but you will be one of the first to meet her."

"Amazing," Lisa said. "I'm packing right now. My plane leaves really early east coast time so I'll be there in the morning tomorrow."

"Lee Axelrad is going to pick you up at the airport, okay? Marley will be with the Axelrad's while we're at the hospital, so just come to us and Mitchel will give you the keys for the house and car."

Lisa arrived at the birthing center just a few hours after Ruby was born. She spent the first night in the hospital sleeping next to Ruby and me on the pull out armchair meant for the new father, but Mitchel went home to sleep with Marley at our house.

"I know why people don't have babies when they get older," she said into the dark room. Ruby had just cried out for a nursing and although I thought I got to her pretty quickly and stuffed my breast in her mouth, she had woken my sister as well.

"What do you mean?" I asked her. I liked having this conversation with her as we lay in our beds in the dark. I had missed out on sharing a room with my sister growing up and always envied the idea of having a conversation between the bunks, but it never happened.

"Well, I don't know if it's my cancer or my age, but I just can't go in and out of sleep like this. And, my body can't get comfortable, ever."

It was the first time I heard Lisa complain about her body, age, or cancer. I was struck by how terrible that would be, to never be able to get comfortable. I felt so far from that experience with my baby snuggled up against me, a cozy pocket of warmth and love between us. Already on Day One, Ruby had developed a habit of tucking her little legs under my arms as she nursed, seeking warmth and connection.

Unlike Marley, this baby girl came out of the womb knowing how to nurse. She loved my milky ways and they were the perfect pillows for the perfect head. Asleep in my arms from the soporific effects of nursing, she would continue the mouth movements of nursing in her sleep. Mitchel and I joked that she was dreaming of booby mountains, those lazy, luscious, rolling hills of love.

Lisa's visit, like all the others, was not long enough, but parting was made a bit easier by the fact that I would be out to Rochester in just three months to celebrate Lisa's 50th birthday. The downtime I had available as Ruby nursed and napped was the perfect chance to plan a party for Lisa's Half Century Celebration. It would be my first time traveling with Ruby on my own, but I would have a lot of help once I got there because all of Lisa's friends were baby crazy, and there was Dylan and Elliott too. I was also looking forward to meeting Charlie, my sister's first real boyfriend after she and Bruce broke up. Charlie was a piano tuner by day and jazz musician in a band at night, which Lisa loved, and he didn't shy away from the relationship when he heard that Lisa's cancer was back after only dating for three weeks.

Instead of presents Lisa requested that everyone come to her house to pitch in and help her implement a basement revision she had been dreaming of for years. She had even entered a home makeover contest a few months before, on her local TV station morning show. Lisa's tragic health story, plus the fact that her compelling desire to do the basement revision was in order to leave the house in good condition for her sons, seem to make her a shoe-in for the prize. When she didn't win, Lisa was at first disappointed, yet upon learning that the winner was a family with an ailing young daughter, she was glad it was going to someone worthy of the prize. Lisa even admitted that while she felt bad saying it, she felt better to know that someone was in a worse situation than she was.

Lisa's hope for the party was that we could gather our collective resources and pull off a small-scale version of the basement remodel plans, as well as scratch the surface on a few odd jobs around the house.

Lisa's house was bustling with people with paintbrushes or screwdrivers in hand starting at 8 in the morning. While everyone knew the true reason for the event, they kept the mood festive. There was music playing, people brought over great snacks, and Lisa was having a blast being the chatty Queen of the party, while all her loving worker bees got busy making her home beautiful.

We broke off into teams to work on different projects. The more technically capable folks tackled the basement, others worked to organize large Tupperware crates of holiday ornaments, outgrown clothes, and extra supplies of Ziploc bags or parmesan cheese that Lisa couldn't help but stock up on during sales at her favorite grocery store, Wegman's. I worked with a crew of mostly teenage friends of Dylan and Elliott, painting the kitchen cabinets. By the end of the day, the house looked half-done. It wasn't exactly the plan Lisa had envisioned, but none-the-less the basement now had a toilet and running water; there was a new washer and dryer, and a nook for folding and organizing laundry. The kitchen was painted bright yellow with orange and green trim to match her Fiesta Ware collection, the joyful colors masking the bottom line reason behind the party—to get Lisa's house in order before she died.

The second part of the party was about relaxing and celebrating. Everyone got cleaned up and headed to a local park for the party. Charlie and his band played great jazz music and everyone danced. Pop got his thrills sweeping Lisa and me across the dance floor. With Pop it was not necessary to know the steps, his solid lead leaving no room for interpretation.

Lisa was thrilled to be surrounded by the love and good cheer of her favorite friends and "special treasures" as she called her team of people that had helped her with doctor's appointments, errands, and other projects over the years. A few times I glanced at Lisa and saw her smiling in a familiar way, but one that I hadn't seen in a while. It was wonderful to see that Lisa was getting this time, falling in love again, being part of her boys' lives, and living.

Later, back at her house, Lisa walked into the upstairs den where Dylan, Elliott, and I were all sitting around the computer and TV.

"Thanks everyone for the great party. The house looks amazing," Lisa said and paused for a moment before declaring, "This is the year of I don't give a flying fuck." I looked over at Dylan and Elliott to see if they reacted to their mom saying the F word. As the mom of two young girls, I was probably overly sensitive to this because neither boy blinked an eye. Lisa sounded relieved, perhaps because of the wine or maybe because she really did feel it was time to let go.

Sadly, the year's theme ended before it really started.

I was up before anyone else the next morning getting Ruby some cereal and fruit when I felt a little drip on my face. Wiping it away I continued getting Ruby's snack together when I felt it again. This time I looked up and saw a stalactite of ceiling plaster looking like it could pierce me. I moved out of the way and then instantly ran toward the basement. That basement was the bane of Lisa's life. It pretty much always flooded at least once each winter, ruining clothes, food, and storage boxes annually. It was perfectly ironic that the new plumbing we put in the day before was already an issue. Finding nothing there I came back upstairs to the kitchen and decided to follow the wetness to its source above me. Toward the top of the staircase the carpet runner covering the stairs began to feel like I was walking on a sponge. Continuing toward the hall bath the dampness increased. As I turned the corner I could see through a crack in the bathroom door that Pop was there, plunger in hand, staring blankly at the toilet, which continued to flow over with water.

"Shut the door fast," he said, trying to trap as much water in the room as possible, though clearly without much success.

If I were to characterize the relationship between my sister and Pop I would call it contentious. My sister pretty much blamed anything that didn't go right in her life on Pop. And Pop didn't think she was doing much right. During Lisa's junior year of high school, when Pop found out she was on the Pill, Pop sent her to a high school in Sweden where she lived with a host family. I think he meant to reform her, but instead she spent the year learning about Swedish boys. Over the years Pop openly disagreed with how Lisa led her life—how she spent money, who she spent time with, the jobs she had chosen given her pedigree, or that she was living in Rochester, New York, with a non-Jewish husband.

There was no telling what he would have to say about this crappy situation. So, with the basement and kitchen remodel from the day before, drenched in the excrement of our father, Lisa's 50's were off to a bad start. And that was just the beginning of the flood our family was about to experience.

CHAPTER 16

HUSH PUPPIES

As a child I always called my dad Papa. While it is more commonly used for a grandfather, perhaps it was because he was older than most "dads" or because he wanted to differentiate his role in my life from that of my siblings, but Papa he was to me up until I was a teenager, when I began calling him the more mature, Pop.

In general, Pop was not involved in the day-to-day of my life. I spent time with my mom, and for the most part, Pop didn't get involved in parenting. But watch out on those rare times when I did something he didn't find appropriate, because then Pop would show me who was boss. My response was to sprint down the hallway, desperate to get ahead of his spanking by going into my bedroom and closing the door.

I don't remember seeing my Mom and Pop argue, though I can't imagine she was immune from his wrath. Pop was always mad at someone, breaking off relationships based on stories he told himself of their infidelities, or for some other reason Pop developed a feeling of mistrust. A lawyer by practice, he was a litigious man through and through, and this played out in how he ran his life, as well as his career. He was like a bloodhound, always searching out his next trial.

The happiest I have ever seen Pop was in the midst of the O. J. Simpson debacle. He loved the daily news clips of what was happening and enjoyed conversations, especially with Mitchel, about how there was not enough evidence to convict him, and that they should find O.J innocent until proven guilty.

I often attributed Pop's curmudgeon-like personality to the failure of his law firm. I was about five years old when it all went down, but the story that was always told to me is that Pop went to work one day at his self-started partnership of Kubby Prichard, Cohen, and Smallhair, and the locks on the door had been changed. Pop could see his colleagues and secretarial staff through the windows, but they would not let him in. According to my dad he had no idea why they had cut him off, and the real story, if there was one, would go with him to his grave.

Pop always seemed to feel that he needed to conform to a mold of a "good man" that stemmed from his childhood. The oldest of three children in his family, neither his brother nor his sister survived beyond the age of four, dying prematurely from Tay Sachs. Pop was left to carry on the Kubby name, holding the torch of hope for their small family. At the age of 18, he left Council Bluffs, Iowa, and went to Stanford, becoming the first in his family to go to college.

After finishing undergrad Magna Cum Laude, Pop decided to pursue a legal degree. One of his fraternity brothers set him up on a blind date at a parlor dance party where he danced the night away with a beautiful debutant, who would become his wife. My mom, who was told she couldn't get married until she graduated college, waited until the day after her graduation to say the I Do's. Since her family was there from Peoria, Illinois anyway, the celebrations were doubled on an uncharacteristically hot summer night at the Sir Francis Drake Hotel, in San Francisco.

They made their first home in Sunnyvale where Pop also set up his shingle as a Civil Rights Attorney. Soon after, my sister Lisa was born, and eighteen months later, my brother Joel.

But while Pop followed a traditional map he believed was the right way, my guess is that at some point he felt there was something missing, something more. So instead of stepping into the unknown, or sharing his feelings with others who could support him, he pulled away from the people who loved and cared for him out of fear of them seeing his real truth. And this made him a bitter and angry man.

No matter what the origin of my father's discontent with life, a black cloud seemed to follow him most of his days. Even though I would characterize my relationship with Pop as pretty good overall, I am often struck by memories I have of my early years when Pop betrayed me somehow.

The first time he let me down was the hardest. I was an admitted thumb sucker. It helped me calm down at the end of the day and offered safe passage toward sleep. I loved to have my thumby between my lips and rub the top of my hand along the bottom of my pillow, its softness and the familiarity of my thumb in my mouth providing me the perfect security and comfort to fall into a deep and peaceful sleep. But I was about to start second grade and had just been invited to a sleep over at Lisa Anderson's house. While my thumb was great within the confines of my bedroom, I didn't like the idea of my friends seeing me do it.

The other thing I didn't like was that Pop smoked cigarettes. While tobacco was still in vogue at that time, I knew somehow that it wasn't good, and I didn't like the smell. Pop had never smoked in the house, or in front of me, but I knew that he did because I smelled it on his blazer when he came home, and there were ashtrays, filled with white stubs and ash, scattered around our large yard and on the balcony of his office suite. But at five years old I didn't have the slightest concept of how hard it would be for him to stop.

One night the smell of smoke on his clothes was so overwhelming that it gave me an idea. "Papa, if I were able to stop sucking my thumb," I said after he had read me a story in bed, "would you stop smoking?" It seemed a fair trade to a girl my age.

"Let's start on the weekend," he said, buying himself a few days to finish the pack of Winstons he had already purchased.

It took me over an hour to fall off to sleep with only my pillowcase to console me. My mom read me three books instead of my usual two because she thought it would help if I were very tired when I tried to fall asleep without my thumb. After Mom turned out my lights I was still awake rearranging my stuffed animals on different shelves and counting the glow-in-the-dark stars Joel had stuck on my ceiling as a gift on my fourth birthday.

The next night I was asleep after counting two hundred and thirty-two sheep, and by the third night, when my mom offered to put the horrible tasting nail polish on my thumb, I declined and attempted to test my will power and go it alone. I awoke from the success the next morning and bounded out of bed with excitement to tell my parents the great news.

Walking down the hallway decorated with family photos I listened for my parents' voices. They would either be sitting at the round dining table in our kitchen with their morning coffee, cottage cheese and the *SF Chronicle*, or already out on the tennis court warming up with some light rallies. As I passed through the empty kitchen and came to the sliding glass door that led out to the porch, I could see Pop's shape outside. He was obscured by the glare of the sun on the window, but it looked like maybe he was talking on the phone.

The noise of the door sliding open got his attention, and as he turned and first took notice of me, he shoved his hand down behind his leg. After a few steps I realized why he made that move. There was smoke coming from the side of his legs and the smell of stale burnt air.

In one swift glance at his eyes I could see the realization that he had let me down. The look on his face was one I would come to understand as shame. I was devastated and felt betrayed by the person in my life who really mattered. I had believed he would try as hard as I would to stop. Suddenly I got a sense of what it meant to disappoint and to be disappointed, and a wedge developed between me and Pop and me, one that would grow with the years as we learned to hide from each other to avoid disappointing and of being disappointed.

Pop's judgments about what was right and wrong were not only focused on me and they weren't all bad. In the late 60's Pop argued for the first black family to become members of our country club, and spent years of his attorney practice litigating civil claims for Asians who had been wronged by the railroads where they had worked.

But other aspects of his black and white vision were less flattering. Being raised by a generation that experienced the Holocaust, Pop took away an unfortunate dislike for all things German. If he heard someone speaking German, he would wrinkle his face and move to another part of the room. When I got my driver's license and was shopping for used cars, Pop told me I could get any make or model except for a Volkswagen. No Cabriolet for me. I even went so far as to never show him the tattoo I got at age 21, since I knew ink on the body reminded him of the numbers imprinted on Jews in concentration camps.

As I grew, Pop kept firm boundaries about what our relationship looked like. I learned to only show him the things that I believed he wanted to see about me – the Varsity swimmer, the honors student, the member of student council, or the prom court beauty. I shined out the parts of me that I knew he would approve of, and shoved to the back the other parts of me that went to Grateful Dead concerts and had sex.

But even given these limitations, I loved Pop for being my papa and he really worked to show up for me in the years after I had my own children. It was clear he wanted to help fill the void of my mom's death and he really stepped up as a grandfather and father. It was surprising how naturally he took on this new title and responsibilities with my kids given his lack of participation in my early years of life.

In honor of his 77th birthday and Father's Day, he had gone online and rented a beach house in Pajaro Dunes for me, Mitchel and the girls, and Joel to enjoy together. I was impressed with his savvy to find the unit on Craig's list. This "new" Pop was a far cry from the man who wouldn't use a cell phone because the numbers were too small and anyway, he didn't want to give them his social security number to get an account. Suddenly he was no longer a curmudgeon. I had not seen Pop looking so healthy, vibrant and alive as he did that weekend. The joy of family seemed to fill his heart, and a realization of how important it was to spend quality time being together seemed to emerge.

After that lovely trip we kept the contact rolling and met up a few weeks later when Lisa was in town, at Fairy Tale Town in Oakland for a fun family outing. Pop was beaming as he carried Ruby from ride to ride—his face, full of the joy only a grandfather can know. There was even a small glimmer of a skip to his step. His olive skin was glowing from a summer of sun, and he looked strong, stable and alive.

The final photo I have of myself with Pop was taken later that day in Oakland. Besides pop and me there are Lisa, Joel, Marley, Ruby, my best friend and her son, and Lisa's best friend, standing in front of a bougainvillea bush. When I look at the photo what I find remarkable is that all three of us Kubby kids shared the same final moment with our dad. I have looked at that image a hundred times to see if I can find a hint of it being our last moments together. I look for an extra bend in Pop's back, or a wince of pain crossing his face. But really what I see is all of us looking like the worst is behind us.

*Pop's (Last) Birthday and Father's Day Celebrations,
Pajaro Dunes, CA. June 2007.*

The last time we all saw Pop. Oakland, CA. August 2007.

CHAPTER 17

KNOCKERS

I was in bed when the doorbell rang. It was 11:18 p.m. and Mitchel and I were settling into our nightly sleep-inducing read. The late hour of an unknown visitor was disconcerting, as was the fact that whoever it was clearly disregarded the sign above the doorbell: "Baby sleeping, please don't ring." Much like a late night phone call, my gut knew that nothing good could come from a middle-of-the-night knock on the door. We waited to see if they'd go away, but when the doorbell was followed by knocks, Mitchel decided it was not a teenage prankster mistaking our house for that of the 15-year-old girl next door.

It was a hot August night, so Mitchel was in boxer briefs. I remember him hastily pulling on a t-shirt and wavering a bit before deciding that was enough clothing given the late hour. I put my book aside and listened to the sound of his footsteps down the hall to the door. I heard the tug of the door and then Mitchel saying, "It's 11 at night. We have children sleeping." A man's voice apologized and asked if Mitchel could open the screen door. Their voices got so hushed I had to strain to hear what they were saying, but it was clear from the tone that something bad had occurred. I imagined there was a fire nearby, or a stray dog. Maybe a neighbor was concerned about a party in one of the college rentals on the street. I tried to sit back and enjoy my book, keeping half an ear to the door. After a few more minutes, I decided to walk down the hall to see what the hassle was about. I caught sight of an unfamiliar man wearing an organizational nametag. Squinting into the darkness I made out the word *Coroner* and instantly I assumed one of Mitchel's patients had committed suicide.

"Is it one of your patients?" I asked.

"No," Mitchel said, turning to me with a sad face, "it's your dad."

I was stunned and stayed on the bench by the front door for almost an hour, not moving before Mitchel encouraged me to come to bed. He offered to tell the girls in the morning so I could be saved that painful experience and suggested that I leave the house before they woke up. This would be the first death they experienced, and my first time mourning a loss with kids that still very much needed me to stay strong.

After a restless sleep, I got up silently and quickly packed up an overnight bag. I didn't even take the time to find something black for the funeral. The mortuary called me on my drive to Palo Alto. "From the decomposition of your father's body that we witnessed, it appears he died at least 5 days ago," a stranger's voice said into my Bluetooth headset and then he told me all the details he knew about what happened. A neighbor at their posh 55 and over condo units had called the manager to say there was a strange smell coming from the unit, and they hadn't seen Pop around in a few days. It appears he had a heart attack alone in the apartment. "I don't suggest you go to the house alone, ma'am, on account of the state of things there."

After this strange conversation I pulled over to get gas and called Joel. He was just coming off Highway 17 at 280 and would be there soon. When I got to Pop's condo I sat in my Subaru and took a stab at Pop's obituary. I would need Joel and particularly Lisa, to help me fill in the blanks of dates, but I got a good start.

When Joel arrived we held each other and I let out the first tears I cried since hearing the news. Our parents were gone, and with Lisa's health being so poor, he and I were really the ones that were left.

Together we took the familiar walk from the parking lot to the entrance gate and put in the code that would buzz us in since nobody was on the other side of the intercom to let us in.

As we crossed by the pool and into the door of Pop's building I called to Joel to take the stairs with me. I wanted to move as slowly as could be at this point. As soon as we entered the hall to Pop's condo, yellow caution tape caught my eye and heart.

"Shall we do it?" Joel asked, and proceeded down the hallway to Pop's door. Everything looked the same on the outside—the basket of dried plants my mom had set out years ago, a welcome mat with two tennis racquets on it, and a *mezuzah* to the right of the door well.

My nose was attacked as Joel opened the door. It smelled rotten and stale at the same time. All the windows had been closed to try to keep out pests, but all it had done was keep the foul air in. Joel walked in first, trying his best to be the big brother and now patriarch. He went to the sliding doors in the living room and began opening everything up.

"Can I come in now?" I yelled from the door, even though I didn't really want to go in.

"Hold on a sec," Joel yelled from inside the condo. When he came to the door a minute later I could see the torture on his face.

"I threw a towel over most of it, but if you can help it, don't look down the hall."

Of course, his saying that only made me look. It is human nature to be drawn toward what people tell us to avoid, but then I saw the pool of blood in the carpet beyond the towel and quickly turned away, wishing I had listened to his suggestion.

"I think we should go to the store and get some fans and cleaning stuff," Joel said, "and let the place air out a bit."

Never will I get out of my head the memory of going to Safeway to buy rug cleaning solvent, bug killing agent, heavy duty gloves, masks, and multi-ply garbage bags to clean up Pop's guts. Joel also threw a box cutter into the basket.

When we returned to the condo Joel worked that area for four hours or more, trying his physics magic to get the stains out of the carpet, until he finally cut out the entire 6 foot by 3 foot piece of Berber carpet. It turns out there are special cleaners for hire for just this situation, but we didn't know about that service and suffered through it ourselves.

Unfortunately the horrors didn't end there. While Joel was dealing with the carpet, I was getting other parts of the house in order. I went through the fridge and tossed out a half-full carton of skim milk, some jack cheese, a head of iceberg lettuce, and some decrepit grapes. I washed the dishes that were by the sink, and started to cry again as I realized this was all that was left of Pop's final meal. Before moving on to sorting all the mail I decided to listen to the messages on his machine. I had called him Sunday, so had Joel, there was a call for a delivery, and also a message from a man who had come to see Pop and was waiting at the gate to be buzzed in.

It turns out that the final message was just the beginning of a lot of evidence suggesting Pop hadn't been lonely all these years. Well, lonely maybe, but alone, not so much. Cleaning up his apartment and clearing out his belongings that day, it became increasingly evident that my father had lived a good part of his life as a gay man. When I went into Pop's office to print the program for his funeral, I was looking for paper and came across several large boxes which seemed like they might contain reams of paper but instead were full of photos of Pop arm-in-arm with men we never heard word of, printouts of AOL emails between Pop and numerous perspective suitors, and even ticket stubs from a gay cruise in Tahiti.

The more I found, the more I became obsessed with finding more; searching to find out about the life of a man that I thought I knew well but didn't know at all.

Suddenly Pop's love of nude beaches and why he was always tan in the middle of November became clearer. It seems he was not always in foggy Half Moon Bay where he said his dark color came from but really on a sun-filled vacation being gay in every sense of the word, while I was worried that I hadn't been seeing him enough and he was sitting in his apartment alone.

My family had occasionally joked about Pop's guy friends over the years—Joe from the Grecian Spa days in Palo Alto was a topic of conversation for years, but never had I considered he was leading such an active double life.

Suddenly I was getting new perspective on a man I thought I had known more than most. Something about all this new information helped shed light on Pop's lifelong anger and resentment. He had been a gay man trying to perform the duties he believed a good husband was meant to do. Sadly, Pop came from a generation where this would not be acceptable. I am sure he thought none-of-us could handle knowing this truth. It was too shameful. He could not be gay and also be loved by his family. I could understand how holding all that in had a toxic effect. In some ways it seemed Pop wanted us to find all this out after he was gone. Like he didn't want to burden us with it, but saw death as a chance to come clean.

What I failed to realize until this point was this tragedy of our relationship—we had been hiding from each other all these years. It pains me to the core that I wasn't given the opportunity to open my arms to him, and accept him fully for who he was, and that he could never do the same for me. I wish I could wrap my arms around him and feel us radiating our deep unconditional love toward each other. I grieve the loss of this opportunity daily.

Yet there are still parts of me that aim to please, even long after his death. I continue to strive to be seen as a great mom, devoted wife, successful entrepreneur, powerful writer, generous volunteer, and a fun loving gal. But there are many moments when I am not – and when the reality of what I am feeling and experiencing is not measured realistically by the smile I try to keep on my face.

But since I can't redo what has happened, and will not have the chance to make it different with Pop, I realize how I can use this to help me live my life differently now. Extrinsic validation is lovely, but not a necessity, and its presence or absence does not define me. To feel truly cherished and whole means that I need to give myself the love and acceptance that will keep me thriving.

The night before Pop's memorial service, Lisa, Joel, and I met with our local rabbi, who was now presiding over the synagogue where I had studied, sang in the choir, and became a bat mitzvah and married. Rabbi Marder had just begun leading the synagogue as my parents separated, and had inspired my mom to turn to Judaism as part of her healing. It seemed we had just been sitting on this same couch talking about my mom's funeral.

"The *Kaddish Yatom*," Rabbi Marder explained about the prayer said by Jewish mourners for a year following the death of a loved one, "is literally translated to mean the 'Orphan's Prayer.'" When she remarked that we were now orphans abandoned at ages 51, 49, and 35, I couldn't believe those words applied to me. I had never thought of the idea of being parentless, or considered what it would feel like. "Orphan" sounded like a word for other people—painful, permanent, and overly mature.

I had already dealt with the death of one parent, but this was an entirely different experience. My mother died slowly over time. I watched her go from a tennis-playing aerobics instructor to a wheelchair-bound, wig-wearing woman over the course of many months. The pain was drawn out, yet I had a chance to process what was happening along the way. I was able to bring closure to our time together as she was fading away from me. The slow pace allowed me time to figure out my next phase as a motherless daughter and what it would mean for who I would become. Saying good-bye came in bits and pieces.

Pop's death felt more like a trauma than I had experienced with my mom's dying. I hadn't expected to lose him when I did. I felt untethered, like a balloon floating off into the sky. I had moments of being consumed with the idea of being nobody's child. There was so much unsaid, so much hiding, and so many conversations that we would never be given the chance to have.

I was sad that Ruby, at the age of three, would not remember her "Pop Zede," and that both girls had lost yet another grandparent. I looked to Lisa and Joel, realizing that they were in the same boat with me. I was sad for us all but also comforted to have them with me as we went through this. They would protect me. They always had.

Feeling as though the final connections to my birth, infancy, and youth were slipping away—I felt drawn to people who knew me as a child, those who knew my parents and my first home. Even though I had been living my life as an adult for years, suddenly I was really a grown-up. A parentless parent—instead of receiving that deep unconditional love, it was now transferred to my arms, heart and soul to deliver to my children.

But besides those moments of sorrow, I was mostly numb—in shock from trying to understand who exactly I was mourning and angry that these new images of Pop were so strong that they were taking over for the 33 years of memories that had been in their place. At the same time I wanted to mourn the loss of the father I did have, one that had loved me and that I loved very much.

I tried to stay focused and not drop too deeply into any of this so that I could make it through the funeral, my speech and the burial before I could completely let down my guard. What I wanted to share at his funeral was that Pop's strong emotions and beliefs, though alienating at times, had guided me through the years and would stay with me beyond his death. Indeed, some of his best lessons have become my own, and these were what I shared at the funeral.

- Believe in good causes
- Get yourself to the beach often
- Help those in need
- Vote
- Appreciate and share what others love and enjoy with them
- Smile with all of your heart
- Don't worry if people turn around when you blow your nose or when you laugh
- Seek out the sun
- Cry when you are happy, often and freely
- Love the underdog
- Dance when you hear music, when you feel a beat, or when you just want to dance, grab someone nearby and dance

CHAPTER 18

TORPEDOES

When my sister told me that her cancer was in her bones, she also told me she was mad that she would die before Pop. As awful as that sounds, I think for Lisa it was the only way to break free from a relationship that had always been troubled, and it was a nice turn of the tides to have his money in her bank account after years of his nagging and fighting over her spending with Pop. With Pop no longer an obstacle, Lisa could also fulfill her yearning to contact Pop's old law partners and find out what happened the day they changed the locks on their office, breaking off the partnership.

Unfortunately Lisa didn't get a long time to bask in the glory of her success. Ironically, just as Lisa was set free of the grip of my father, her health started going downhill simultaneously with his death. A few weeks after Lisa returned for the funeral, she started having some numbness in her arms and legs. Several tests and MRIs later it was diagnosed that Lisa's cancer had spread to her brain, affecting her neurology. They scheduled her to begin having a radial surgical treatment once a week where a laser gamma knife would cut away at the tumors in her brain. On one visit Lisa was even excited to show me the headgear that was designed just for her head so that the radiation could be precisely delivered. Lisa had a beautiful optimism about the effectiveness of this treatment that quickly vanished when her symptoms persisted. It was unclear if it was the progression of the disease or the treatment that was causing Lisa new issues, but she seemed to start having "episodes" more and more regularly.

The biggest scare came when Lisa was alone with Dylan and Elliott walking through the mall, buying things the boys needed for school and sports, when Lisa suddenly fell to the ground. When the boys picked her up, she wasn't able to walk unless she was huddled over staring at the ground. Something was the matter with her balance and combined with the numbness in her legs it became hard for her to stand.

I made an emergency trip back east. It felt good to be there to support Lisa and the boys and help take care of some of the day-to-day tasks that were becoming hard for Lisa to manage. Mostly I spent time around her house, sorting, organizing, and creating systems to help the days flow more smoothly as I often had done on my trips to Rochester, knowing from experience that it would fall back to chaos a few days after I left.

Lisa and I had some very real conversations about what was next as she was now feeling like her life wasn't going to be much longer. There were important tasks that now felt urgent. She had recently hired a lawyer to get her will and trust in place, and, since I would be the Executor, she wanted me to meet with her. She also wanted to put labels with people's names behind certain pieces of art that she wanted to pass along when she died. I was struck by Lisa's relative acceptance and positivity as we went through these final preparations.

I was also going through a transition of sorts during my time in Rochester, although I hadn't planned it that way. Since this had been an emergency trip and I wasn't sure what Lisa would need when I arrived, I had come to Rochester without either of my girls. Though it would only be four days it was the longest I had been away from Ruby since she was born, and she was still nursing sporadically. I made a conscious decision when I left that

I wasn't going to bring a pump, so the only milk left was what we had frozen at home. By the second day my breasts had gotten very sore, and swollen, and then a bit hard. It seemed my milk was starting to dry up from not being used which meant ending the days of my life as a lactating woman. I felt ready in many ways, although I was mourning this loss as well.

A happier part of the trip was how much time Lisa and I shared in her room cuddling, reminiscing and giggling. At moments I felt like her bed was a time machine, transporting us back 20 years where we lay side by side in her waterbed, no wrinkles from worry in our brows, no scars across Lisa's chest, our mom alive, and a sense of possibility and hope for the future that alluded us now.

I dreaded having to say good-bye to Lisa. I knew well from my experience with my mom that at this stage of the disease, you could never know what state the person would be in at the next visit. Changes were coming daily. Even after a lifetime of good-byes between us they never got easier. This time it was Lisa who pretended to be asleep as I slipped from the room and into the early morning air to grab a taxi to the airport.

I called Lisa the minute I got home to let her know that I arrived safely. "I'm back, Lis. Thanks for the great visit."

"Thank you, Ray Ray. It was really special to have you and I appreciate all the things you took care of around the house."

"Guess what? Ruby pushed through the week not nursing. Sounds like it was a bit hellish for Mitchel, mostly the nights, but, I don't think we'll go back now."

"Wow, Ray, that is big," Lisa said. "I already miss you so much. I found your "Tree Hugger" t-shirt in the laundry basket. I'll send it along in a few days."

I didn't remind her that her doctor had ordered her not to drive anymore but instead offered her a little bit of hope.

"I'm going to make a call about getting tested, Lis. I'm ready, it's time," I said, relieved to have shared this with her.

So just like that, the sweetness of my nursing days dried up and I moved on to the next chapter of my breast's story as I faced-down my family history of breast cancer.

Us four girls. Lisa, Marley, Ruby and me. 2007

PART II

STACKED

scar

we will learn
to live together.
i will call you
ribbon of hunger
and desire
empty pocket flap
edge of before and after.
and you
what will you call me?
woman i ride
and who cannot throw me
and i will not fall off.

-Lucille Clifton

CHAPTER 19

TIME BOMBS

My breasts served me well through the years, though they had a rough start. Being the first girl in the sixth-grade class at Bullis Elementary School to get a bra was not the fame I was looking for at 11 years old. Sure, I read, "Are You There God? It's Me, Margaret," and had the requisite knowledge that the other girls in the room were not far behind, but I was still embarrassed to stick out.

The bottom line of my "top line" is that my "two girls" had provided sustenance to my children; even on days when I am sure they were sore and tired. They had filled out the various push-up bras I had stuffed them into and looked pretty peeking out of plenty of v-neck dresses and halter-tops. They had done their job, and done it well.

So, at 33 years old, two babies birthed and about 3,650 hours of breast-feeding later, I was ready to consider genetic testing.

Making the appointment with the genetic counselor turned out to be an easy step. Our phone conversation was short and logistical covering a basic family history and my referring doctor's information. We set a date two weeks later at a time when Mitchel would be able to join us. Lynn, the genetic counselor let me know that our first meeting would include a detailed listing of my family history and asked that I gather as much information as I could to prepare.

The gravity of this appointment didn't hit home until I was walking into the building, right past a huge sign that read, Sutter Cancer Center. The word CANCER jumped out at me like a fiery blaze of fear. Multi-colored daisies surrounding the cement sign looked like a bright, cheery Mardi Gras mask covering the ugly face of what was in store for those who entered. This was not a place I wanted to become familiar with.

A woman just inside the entrance showed us to the administrative offices. We sat at the first desk in a room full of open cubicles surrounded by shelves and shelves of files. While we waited for our representative to come to talk with us I imagined the many stories and tragedies that the files held, and soon mine would be one of them.

"My name is Ms. Nelson," a woman in a blue business suit said and sat across from us at the desk. "How do you plan to pay for your visit today, Mrs. Adler?"

I was shocked to have a medical appointment that was so personal in nature start here in the financial sector of the medical center. It seemed so impersonal and too much like a business transaction. This was my life and death we were talking about and that didn't have a price tag.

Mitchel jumped in. "Can we wait until after our appointment to decide if we want to pay for this out of pocket or through insurance?"

Ms. Nelson's eyebrows furrowed into a question mark, making it clear she was hearing this request for the very first time. *Cancer patients probably don't have the luxury of deciding how they will pay for treatments,* I thought to myself. We were coming from a unique and strangely privileged situation where we were trying to catch a disease before it took its toll. Surely this would cost the health system a lot less than if I were to get cancer and go through the system that way. It was slowly becoming clear that genetic health issues and the repercussions of choices based on them were a very new and foreign set of issues for the healthcare system.

After leaving the administration area we were ushered over to the Sutter Cancer Center Risk Program in the corner of the 1st Floor, where a receptionist greeted us and asked that we fill out some paperwork while we waited. I barely had a chance to fill the form out when a large-framed woman wearing all white came into the waiting room and introduced herself as our Genetic Counselor and motioned for us to follow her down a hallway. Down the hallway, the counselor pushed open a door to reveal something more akin to a classroom than a medical office, with a round table in the center and wipe erase boards on two of the walls.

The three of us did an awkward shuffle before settling into our seats. The perfunctory introductions revealed that the geneticist, Lynn, had recently moved to California with her husband and two kids and was living in our hometown of Davis.

"I see you have a daughter the same age as mine," Lynn stated. "Where does she go to preschool?"

"Applegate," Mitchel chimed in.

"How about yours?" I asked.

"She is at Rivendell and I have a son in the second grade at César Chavez."

I smiled. "We will send our daughter there next year."

It felt good to connect with Lynn on this level before getting into what was sure to be harder material ahead. I found it comforting that the woman who would tell my health fortune would also be somehow involved in the story as it played out.

Putting the chitchat to the side, we got into my family tree and story. Lynn was reading off the family history I prepared for this meeting. As she went through each relationship she would jot down either an x (female) or 0 (male) on a special sheet of paper. A diagonal slash went through the mark for any relative that was deceased. The process was disturbing, though I am not sure if it was due to the sheer number of slashes she was making, or the way that she would robotically repeat each piece of information as she created the diagram. "Sister, breast cancer, left breast at age 36, right breast at 44. Mother, unilateral breast cancer at 62, melanoma at 68, and lung cancer at 68. Died at 69." SLASH. "Mother's maternal first cousin, unilateral breast cancer at 69. Died at 72." SLASH. "Believe maternal great-grandmother, unilateral breast cancer. Age of death not known." SLASH. "Paternal grandmother, lung cancer at 54, died same year." SLASH. "Father's paternal first cousin, cancer of vena cava at 22, is now 51."

We spent a lot of time on Lisa's history since she was the only person in my family to have been tested for the BRCA gene. Lynn reviewed the letter I brought with the results of Lisa's genetic test. She talked about what this could mean for me in terms of likelihood of also having inherited the gene, as well as the possibilities of false positives, and of my different options depending on what my result showed.

At some point along the way Lynn's voice took on the "wa-wa" sound of the teacher in a "Peanuts" episode and I wasn't able to follow the conversation as it became too overwhelming to take in. Mitchel brought up our concern about insurance coverage and both being self-employed. We were fearful of the possibility of being denied coverage in the future based on a positive test result being seen as an "existing condition." Lynn showed us a map of the U.S. that outlined which states consider genetic predispositions as a covered service and luckily California was one of them. While it was hard for either of us to trust that this wouldn't hurt us, in the end we decided to submit the bill to insurance. My thought process was this: If I got a positive result I would likely go ahead and have surgery, which we wouldn't be able to pay for on our own anyway, so we would need our insurance. If we got a negative result then there was no concern with insurance anyway.

Lynn summarized our meeting and said, "Given your family history and your Ashkenazi Jewish descent, my suggestion to you would be to get tested."

"Okay," I said, ready to dive right in. Coming into today's meeting I had assumed that blood testing was a given so it didn't seem a far stretch to me to do it.

Mitchel took my hand and turned to me. "How would it be for you if we waited a bit?" I looked at him a bit confused by his question. *Didn't he just hear what Lynn had said?* "I'd just like to let this all sit a bit. Is that okay?" He wanted time to think about what a positive or a negative result would mean, and whether or not we were ready to even face the next set of questions. I understood where he was coming from and that all of this had tremendous impacts on him as well. Still, I couldn't help but think that this was so typical of both of us—me, to want to take life by the horns and live in the moment, and Mitchel, to want to take time to process all the different aspects of the situation. While Mitchel and I were more alike than not, there were certain times, like our pace at decision making, where we were more like the Lucy and Desi Arnaz of the new millennium.

Lynn walked us out of the center, thanked us for meeting with her, and handed me a packet of information to peruse as I made my decision. On the top of the pile was a newsletter on salmon paper from a group called FORCE – Facing Our Risk of Cancer Empowered. The turquoise ribbon in the logo was a non-pink surprise. I nodded my head indicating that I would read it. Though I didn't know it at the time, Lynn was throwing me a lifeline by introducing me to FORCE that day.

Mitchel and I walked out of the building and into the clear early spring air. I noticed again the Sutter Cancer Center sign, the flowers and all the people waiting for the valet. Somehow it all seemed less foreign than just an hour earlier. We walked silently for a block hand-in-hand. I squeezed Mitchell's palm in mine like a child not wanting to let go of her balloon. And then, just before arriving at the parking lot and our car, he turned to me and said, "I think we should do it."

Two weeks later we were back at Sutter to get our results. I knew the answer as soon as we checked in. Lynn was at the computer doing some paperwork and seemed surprised by the fact that we were about 10 minutes early for our appointment. "Uhhh, have a seat guys," she mumbled, barely turning her eyes away from the computer screen to great us "I'lllllll be right with you." Now, this was not the greeting of someone who is excited to tell me some very happy news. Rather, someone who knows she will be seeing us daily in the halls of our shared elementary school and is mortified that she will have to watch me have cancer daily. I don't even need to go into the room to hear the words. It is written all over her face. When we are finally sitting, there is a quick shuffle of papers and then Lynn lets the words sprint out of her mouth. "TheresultscamebackpositiveforBRCA2mutation" all spilled out in one big jumble. Mitchel placed his forehead into his hands and said "shit," and then the room went silent as I gathered my battle gear, preparing for the fight that I now knew was ahead. The target moved front and center. My positive result was validation of what I already knew, and in some ways, motivation to do something about it.

"I'm so sorry," Lynn said with a pained look on her face. "The good news is that you have so many options for what you do next."

She shuffled some papers and pulled out a light blue paper with my test results and set it down between Mitchel and me.

"Yours is the BRCA2 mutation. The same one Lisa had. This means you have a 56 to 84 percent chance of developing breast cancer over your lifetime, and a 16 to 27 percent chance of developing ovarian cancer," Lynn said in a way I could tell she had rattled off these statistics before. I had always thought of myself as high-risk, but this was over the top.

"You have a lot of options for the level at which you can respond," she continued to get the facts out. "At a minimum it will require you to do a higher level of surveillance. This will mean alternating between getting either a mammogram or an ultrasound at six-month intervals." I had never had an MRI before, and my history of getting mammograms every three years was already stressful so this was hard to imagine, but I kept listening.

"The next level after surveillance is surgery," Lynn said. "For the breasts the option is bilateral mastectomy. Research shows this option reduces your risk by at least 90 percent. That's less risk than the average woman on the street."

Having always felt myself the biggest risk, this was a nice perspective.

"For the ovaries," Lynn said, "surveillance is a yearly transvaginal ultrasound and a CA-125 blood test. The surgical route is bilateral salpingo-oophorectomy where they remove both your ovaries and fallopian tubes, which can reduce ovarian cancer risk by 96 percent and also reduce the risk of breast cancer to 54 percent without a mastectomy.

This was a lot to think about. I asked Lynn for water to buy myself a moment alone with Mitchel to process it all. When Lynn came back she talked a bit about hormone prevention like Tamoxifen and Arimidex and about the risk I also now had for a second primary cancer as well as a list of other cancers related to BRCA2.

Our ducks in a row, Lynn gave us names of doctors to follow up with—Medical Oncologists, Surgical Ob/Gyns, and Plastic Surgeons. Then she told me more about FORCE.

"FORCE coined the term "Previvor," as a way to name people who have a predisposition to a life-threatening disease. This was new territory," Lynn said, "you should check out the resources they have for people like you."

I felt like I was being inducted into a club that I was not so sure I wanted to join. At the same time I was relieved to realize I was not alone. There were others like me, and they were organized. Welcome to the Previvor Sorority.

As we were closing up our appointment Lynn said something about how there was research suggesting that while a woman's quality of life sometimes takes a dip after getting a positive result, one year later most women found they had an even higher quality of life than before they tested. I understood she said this to console me, but the idea repelled me. Why did my quality of life need to dip? What if this result could be more like a get-out-of-jail-free card than a death sentence?

Although statistically I had a very high chance of developing breast cancer, now I could actually do something about it and have my insurance support my choices.

Ever the optimist, I left the appointment with a big to do list of research, doctor to meet, and choices to make.

I was on a mission to disarm the ticking time bombs in my chest.

CHAPTER 20

BOOBY TRAPS

Walking away from my genetic testing with a positive result, I felt like the first chapter of my "choose your own adventure" life was before me. I was now the author of "**Raychel's Booby Trap Adventure.**" At the end of this chapter, two choices would be offered for how to proceed:

If you decide to fight the dragon, turn to page 4.

If you decide to visit the sorcerer, turn to page 5.

As the plot thickened, the choices evolved, and depending on the paths chosen along the way I would experience one of multiple possible endings.

In my hands were a bunch of brochures and business cards telling me about plastic surgeons, gynecological oncologists, breast surgeons, and programs and organizations to support a person making a choice like I was making. Some of them were local to the Sacramento Area and others were across the country or state.

The next few weeks I used all my resources emailing, calling and reading a ton to try to get the decision process rolling. I felt like a teenage boy who couldn't stop talking about boobs. I was all consumed. I developed a database to keep track of what I was learning, full of questions to ask people, the various surgical options, and resources and references to follow on my journey.

Would I deal with my breasts and the ovaries, or just focus on the breast piece since it was most relevant to me? Should I continue for a while with just increased surveillance methods? Could I handle having an MRI or mammogram every six months? Should I just cut to the chase and go right for surgery? If I went for surgery, would I want my breasts to be au natual or implants? If natural tissue, what kind of reconstruction method would I choose? A tram of tissue, which would be used to reconstruct the breast, could be taken from many parts of the body such as the buttocks, inner thigh, and abdomen or back and there were free trams and attached. If I decided on implants, should I fill them with silicone or saline?

My options were dizzying, and each had unique benefits and drawbacks. My overwhelm sent me to the FORCE website where I scanned through the various lists and topics to try to get some suggestions for where to start. I was able to quickly gather a few things, most helpful of which was to get myself a copy of Kathy Stilego's Breast Reconstruction Handbook, which became my "Lonely Planet" guide to breast surgery and more over the next few months. Based on my gut feelings and some of the pros/cons of different surgical options presented in the book, I gathered I was most likely a candidate for breast reconstruction using a natural tissue flap. I consider myself a pretty natural girl and the idea of a foreign body in my chest didn't hold appeal. Of course, the aesthetic of round, full, breasts that defied six years of breastfeeding and 36 years of gravity sounded perky, but I just couldn't imagine being 60 years old with breasts lifted up toward my sagging neck.

The DIEP flap was the ultimate "mommy makeover." Get rid of my tummy, lift up my saggy breasts and best of all, end up with new, revised, special edition boobs, free from the worry of cancer. Plus, since I hadn't had breast cancer or breast cancer treatments like radiation, I was a good candidate for a new technique allowing for the skin and/or the nipple to be spared.

When I started to have conversations with friends about this choice the reactions I got made it clear that what seemed obvious to me was not so apparent to others. Reactions ranged from, "But you're not even sick," or "That sounds pretty drastic," all the way to "Well we're all going to die from something."

So I began to turn my sharing and questioning to women with a BRCA mutation. On the web boards for FORCE I found thousands of women who were making or had made these same choices based on their family history and a feeling I was very familiar with of being the next one. It was interesting to note that women who had watched a loved one suffer from ovarian cancer were the ones who went first toward prophylactic ovarian removal, while others, like me, that had watched the torture of breast cancer were quicker to jump on prophylactic mastectomy.

Once I decided that breast reconstruction using a natural tissue flap and a skin and nipple sparing technique was going to be my preferred option, the next choice in my adventure was to find a doctor. On the FORCE website I found a way to search for doctors based on surgical specialty. I plugged in the newest method of breast reconstruction, the DIEP flap, knowing it was also the least practiced. The innovators of this method of reconstruction were on the East Coast, one in New York and one in South Carolina. They were the most reputable and also had the operation and recovery down to a science, including offering a "recovery hotel" to patients who traveled a distance to do the surgery. Given I had two young children to think about, combined with the potential challenges of postoperative care and recovery from a distance, I decided to cross off that option. My search yielded two surgeons who performed DIEP flap in Northern California. Both were well versed in the surgery and had their primary practices in San Francisco. I set up appointments to visit with them each in July.

Dr. Kristi Hear's office was impressive from the moment we walked in. It didn't look medical at all. There was grandeur to the

Mitchel's hand went to his head and he took a few breaths to think. "You mean half of the cost of the surgery isn't covered."

"That's right," said Dr. Hear, "although sometimes you can appeal the portion Diamond charges."

"But there is no guarantee?" Mitchel asked.

"Right. You can talk with Valerie my scheduler about that when you take her your surgery paperwork."

"Can we check a date but not confirm it until we find out?"

"You can check the date, but I don't think you can get confirmation on whether or not they will grant an appeal until after the fact."

Mitchel and I looked at each other bewildered and annoyed. I wondered why she hadn't brought this up earlier. It seemed obvious that most people would be concerned over the costs of the surgery. And to say she ALWAYS works with a partner did not leave a lot of room for her to consider just doing it on her own, or with someone who actually took insurance. Mostly I just wished she had told us this before she wooed us with her beautiful plastic surgery center. At that point I pretty much decided she wasn't my person. One look at Mitchel and I could tell he was on the same page. She lost big points with us for that move, but we still had to meet the other surgeon before making any choices.

We talked with the scheduler on the way out to see if some of the December dates we were considering for surgery would work for Dr. Hear.

"Even if I find a date in our computer that works for Hear, we have to check it against Diamond's office also so I can't give you an answer right now."

"Oh, okay," Mitchel said. "What do you think about the chance of us getting the cost of the surgery on Diamond's side appealed?"

"I think you'd probably get it," she said, "but I've seen people not be cleared too and they have to pay. Do you want me to call over to Dr. Diamond's office to see if they can get you in to see him soon?"

"We are here from Davis for the day so if there is a chance he could see us today it would be good," Mitchel said.

We had an appointment in the afternoon with the other San Francisco DIEP Plastic Surgeon at the same building, but we didn't want to say it while we were in Hear's office. We could probably slip in the appointment with Dr. Diamond.

The meeting with Dr. Diamond was very medical compared to Dr. Hear and all around pretty unimpressive. His specialty was hands, not breasts, and he kept forgetting I didn't have cancer, which made me feel he hadn't had much exposure to BRCA patients. Several times he said things about the surgery being complicated by a breast cancer diagnosis, which can compromise the skin, which made me think he didn't even realize that my surgery was prophylactic. I was not feeling he was my guy.

Luckily, Dr. King's office hit a chord, as it was a blend of the sterile medical space of Diamond's clinic and the lushness of Hear's office. He had some comfy chairs and a decent looking waiting room, although his exam room was not noteworthy.

The beginning of our appointment was pretty much the same as the others. Mary, Dr. King's PA, who looked way too young to be out of college let alone medical school, asked some basic family history questions and probed us a bit about our thoughts on what type of breast surgery we were considering. Mary went out of the room and must have immediately updated Dr. King who walked in a few minutes later. His look matched his name. He had a soft, teddy bear quality to him, and his face and fashion were very "Men's Health" magazine. His eyes looked translucent, which made me feel he was trustworthy and well meaning. And while he acknowledged the aesthetic possibilities of the surgery, he seemed mostly focused on my health and well being, at least at first.

We talked out the basics similar to my appointment with Dr. Hear. Dr. King talked about the great amount of experience he had with DIEP surgeries and explained some of the technical details of breast reconstruction. Clear on the ins-and-outs of microsurgery, we asked Dr. King about the different options to consider when thinking about breast surgeries, which sent him on his next diatribe. All of the sudden he started writing notes and diagrams on the waxy paper covering the exam table that outlined the whole history of breast surgeries. Suddenly he looked like a crazy professor making charts and outlines all over the table like it was his blackboard.

I found it strange and a bit off-putting that although we had come to Dr. King specifically because of his background in DIEP, he seemed to be shifting the conversation toward implant surgery.

"Implants aren't on the table," I said finally, after waiting for him to go on for a few minutes too long about them.

"I really want the DIEP flap surgery," I said.

Dr. King looked at me, seemingly surprised I had cut him off and also a bit ashamed, like he just realized what he had been doing—pushing implants on me. After a silent pause, he came to, and suggested I put on the gown lying on the table.

"Mary and I will come back in a moment to do a physical exam."

I slipped on the blue paper gown, wishing it were Dr. Hear's robe, and moved over to the exam table.

"So," I said to Mitchel, "what do you think?"

"That was quite a dog and pony show there," Mitchel replied.

"Yeah, what was that all about?" I asked.

There was a knock at the door and Dr. King come back in, this time with Mary, and proceeded to tell us that with microsurgery it is important to have two surgeons. I was ready for him to drop a bomb like Dr. Hear had done and say that his partner surgeon would not be covered by our insurance, but instead Dr. King told us that Mary was his partner in the surgery, which only surprised us in that she looked too young to possibly be a surgeon.

"Can you lie back on the table?" Mary asked me. "And put your arms up under your head. Good."

I lay in that awkward position for a few moments and grimaced through Dr. King taking a look at my breasts and gently squeezing them like I was a package of Charmin. Then he cupped them both and moved them upwards and down again against my chest wall.

"Okay. How about you stand up for me now," Mary said.

My gown was open down the middle exposing a full frontal view to Mitchel as well as Dr. King and Mary. With a gesture indicating I scoot up the table, Dr. King proceeded to grab a slab of fat from my abdomen, gave Mary a knowing look and said, "This should do just fine, don't you think?"

Mary nodded her head yes. This exchange was a huge blow to my self-esteem, right in the gut. It was barbaric and embarrassing the way he grabbed my flesh.

"Just don't lose any weight between now and the surgery," Dr. King said, slowly redeeming himself by suggesting it was good I had the tissue available or the DIEP surgery may not have been an option.

Before leaving we met with Dr. King's scheduler Angie, who confirmed that Dr. King was part of our insurance network and set up a date for the surgery.

"Here is a pre-op kit that goes over some of the details you should know before surgery. Don't take any Ibuprofen products for two weeks before the surgery and you can't eat or drink anything after midnight the night before. There is a ton of other information in there too," Angie said as she pointed to a folder she had given me and handed me an appointment card.

It seemed I had made my "choice." I had turned to page 5 and would visit the sorcerer and move forward with prophylactic bilateral mastectomy and reconstructive surgery. I was choosing this for myself rather than living in a place of constant concern for what might come to be. I turned to page 5 and picked hope over fear.

CHAPTER 21

UNIBOOB

My distaste for running can be traced back as far as 5th grade when my fellow 11-year-old buddies and I were required to run a mile for the Governor's Physical Fitness Test. The only thing worse was the embarrassment of the chin up and pull up tests. My peers would stand on the blacktop surrounding the bar and mock those of us whose body weight to upper body strength ratio kept us grounded. Those were the days of my dreadful nickname "Chubby Kubby," that would define a part of my psyche.

Although not a runner, I have always been athletic. I started swimming at the age of two, when, as my parents tell it, they tossed me around in the Hawaiian ocean to see what I could do. Soon the water became my second home. I can still smell the warm chlorine in the air of Ms. Lydia's indoor bubble pool where I took my first lessons and loved diving for rings or coins in the deepest depths of the pool.

My other favorite place is on a bike. It doesn't take much more than wind in my face to remind me of my aqua banana seat bike and matching streamers waving in the breeze as I raced down Palo Hills Drive with Jennifer Chu. In college, I gave up a car for a bike, and in graduate school I began teaching indoor cycling classes as a way to earn cash while enjoying time in the saddle. I have even ventured into the sport of sprint triathlons as an adult.

Although those events involve running, I'm able to sustain the sprint by the adrenaline rush of the swim and bike legs of the race.

So I surprised myself when I decided to complete a half marathon.

I had been searching for the perfect ritual to mark this rite of passage when my sister was dying and I was about to be given a new lease on life. It seemed a great time to set a baseline of my body's capabilities before the *real* race ahead—a chance to take my current body out for a final drive. My neighbor, Dafna, planted the idea of running a course along the coast of Monterey, adding that we could have time to connect by training together. *Anything is possible with the ocean at my side*, I thought to myself before learning that the race was 13 miles, twice as far as I'd ever run before—but already the goal was born.

Around week four when I built up to running six miles, something switched. Running half of my 13-mile goal became a regular workout. The miles started to pile on and I was a running machine. I added the perfect pacing songs to my iPod and mapped out 6 to 10-mile loops through Davis, learning of new nooks and crannies in the town that I thought I already knew. By the beginning of November I had bursitis and several cortisone shots under my belt and was ready to rock out the Big Sur Half Marathon.

On our final run before tapering to prepare for the race, Dafna and I did a mental run-through of race day. We considered several scenarios: What would happen if one of us had to make a pit stop? What would we do if one of us got hurt or needed to walk? We agreed we would stay together—no one left behind.

But even with the best-laid plans, I never ran a step of the race with her.

Race day morning was a blur of excitement, jitters, and protein bars. Dafna and I slipped out of our hotel rooms, perused the continental breakfast for bananas and carbs, and pinned each other's bibs to our shirts in the hotel lobby. As we ventured out, we merged with streams of fit looking people wearing all colors of wicking fabric all walking the half-mile to the race start. Once there we examined our competition, grabbed some goo from the vendors and chugged water in hopes of making one final pee before the race. After the 15 minutes it took to get through the porta potty line, it was time to get ourselves to our starting area.

Perhaps it was my nerves, or the cup of coffee and energy bar breakfast, but just as we got ourselves lined up and started stretching, I needed to poop. Not wanting to add pre-race stress for Dafna, I told her to stay put and that I would come back and get in line with her. But when I returned to what I believed was our spot, my friend wasn't there.

An overhead speaker announced that the first heat of runners would get started in a minute. Looking out over the sea of bodies in front of me, everyone blended together. Panicking, I called out Dafna's name and asked others to do the same. When there was no reply I started to doubt whether I could do the race on my own.

Taking a few clearing breaths, I looked at the pictures pinned to my shirt. Lisa and my mom were beaming up at me. I let myself feel the crowd and the energy of the race. Soon enough I was moving, my feet barely touching the ground as I was carried along by the mass of people. As space appeared around me, I started to pick up my pace to a jog. My race had begun.

The first mile flew by thanks to a good endorphin rush and even better people watching. With the Mile 1 marker to my back I was heading into the first incline. This hill would take me toward the downtown area of Monterey, the Aquarium, and the last bits of suburbia before we hit the coast for the rest of the run. The streets along Cannery Row were lined with crowds of spectators, small bands, and even a person in a sea lion suit, all offering good cheer and best wishes for the race. The most extraordinary salute came during a short run through a tunneled underpass where the sound of live bagpipes reverberated over and over again in a strange echo of music.

As the miles stretched into the fourth and fifth mile and the distractions and cheers came farther and fewer between, I tucked in my ear buds and let my "Music Marathon" playlist take over for inspiration. Songs like "Move Along" by the American Rejects or Cake's "The Distance," set a strong pace and helped the miles float away. I started to feel like it was meant to be that I run alone. This was my journey to take.

I ran faster than I ever have in my life. At each mile marker there was someone with a stopwatch calling out split times. When I kept hearing splits like 9:33 I figured the times were a bit off, or not calibrated by when we each began the race. My training run averaged ten-minute miles.

At mile six I got the perfect second wind when I saw my family. Mitchel, Marley, Ruby, and Dafna's husband and kids all stood from the curb, lifted their signs in the air and sang out, "Come on mama! Come on!"

"We'll see you on the way back," Mitchel said, "Mile 11." Their smiles and songs were just the lift I needed. As if they had given me wings I flew forward knowing I would see them again.

When I circled back along the second half of the course I finally caught site of Dafna at a water station on the other side of the path. She must have been at about mile 6, just after seeing our families. I called out to her and we waved to one another. That was the only time I saw her during the race.

At 2 hours and 5 minutes I crossed the finish of my first half marathon without anyone I knew around to see my finish. There was something right about finishing this race alone, yet surrounded by so many people. As I walked back to the hotel, the rain, which had held off my whole race, sprinkled down over my hot elated body. I was a fire of endorphins, sore muscles, and hope. Nothing could stop me. I was ready for whatever marathons were ahead.

Big Sur Half Marathon, 2008.

CHAPTER 22

MONEY MAKERS

The plan was to have one more fun weekend before surgery, and my annual women's yoga retreat weekend was just the ticket. Twice a year a group of ladies from Davis and the East Bay, travel to Mendocino to the Hearts and Hands retreat house near the coast for a weekend of yoga, knitting, books, nature, exercise, relaxation, and great meals. A hallmark of the yoga retreats was that since each person only had to make one part of a meal the whole weekend, everyone broke out their signature dish.

Saturday night after a delicious dinner of Indonesian potato and cabbage soup by Lucinda and "Yum Yum Good Enchiladas" by Leah, I sat with Shani on the worn green-velvet couch digesting. I was pretty spent after a day of two yoga sessions, making a pot of soup lunch for the crew, taking a hike with Leah through the sand dunes, and a soporific dinner. I was ready for some wine and socializing when Shani turned to me and asked, "Do you want to do an I-Ching reading?"

"Sure," I said, thinking it would be a fine way to spend the evening. I had heard of the I-Ching by name, but didn't really know what it was about. "Is that like a fortune telling?"

"Sort of," Shani said. "The I-Ching is one of the most ancient Chinese texts. Some people call it the Book of Changes and believe it can foretell the future. You ask a question and the I-Ching gives you a 360-degree view of your life." She opened up the book on her lap and handed it to me.

"The I-Ching centers on the ideas of the *dynamic balance of opposites*, the *evolution of events as a process*, and *acceptance of the inevitability of change*," I read to myself. It sounded like something that I could use in this spiritual limbo with my sister dying and my surgery less than a month away. I was ready to accept the inevitability that things were about to change.

"Okay, so how do we start?" I was intrigued.

"A reading involves tossing three coins six times and recording the number of heads and tails. The hexagram pattern gives you an answer to your question. Ask an open ended question," Shani said, getting things rolling. "Have it be about something that's preoccupying you right now. The time frame should be over the next few weeks or months. Also, make sure you ask the question that's the one you are thinking of because the I-Ching will answer the question in your mind."

"Hmm, let's see. I think the question is something like, 'How can I be the best with my body the next month and how will it change over the coming year?'"

"Okay, good question, let's write it down," Shani said pulling out a pencil and a small spiral notebook with a purple and black geometric design on the cover. "I'm going to start your coin toss now. You should think about your question while I'm tossing."

I wondered as she pulled out her coins if I had indeed asked my real question or if there was something more real and important I should have asked. Shani began to toss the coins and make marks with each throw. She started at the bottom of the page and worked her way up. Toss. Write. Toss. Write.

Once she was done with the tossing and had her notes Shani mumbled to herself while looking up the I-Ching pattern in her book. "Broken, straight, broken," she said more to herself than to me. Shani looked up and into my eyes. "That's intense Raychel. I've never seen that before. You have no changing lines."

"What? What does that mean?" I asked, trying not to get too freaked out without knowing what I should be freaked out about.

"It's just really unusual with six changes possible. I guess it means that nothing is moving—nothing is changing. I don't know what it means specifically, but we should see how it relates to your reading and your question."

"You're a 60," Shani announced and took a breath before reading aloud my hexagram's meaning. "This is Chieh - Restraint-Limitation. Water over Lake," she read from the book. "If you know and respect your personal limits, you will have greater freedom of expression within them. It is wise to restrain the desires and fears that are the cause of troubled thinking. Self discipline teetering toward self-destruction. An empty martyrdom. Turn back."

There were quite a few elements of this fortune that would swim in my head for days, but the words "turn back" imprinted in my brain. I tried to keep myself from panicking, but these were not the words I wanted to hear.

Knowing that Shani would never intentionally be callous, I was surprised when she said, "I keep thinking about the fact that you've got no changing lines and that means that there was no future." A wave of panic hit for a few seconds thinking that meant I was about to die.

I had felt the call of death only one other time in my life. It was during my pre-wedding massage at Ohrr hot springs when I saw a white light and a vision of my spirit body looking down on me as I was dying. That time, I hadn't felt scared, only sad that my time had come before my wedding. This time was not so peaceful.

I pushed Shani to explain it more but she didn't have an explanation. We were both overwhelmed by what had transpired, so we called it a night. "More yoga in the morning," I said as I left the room, trying to sound normal even though part of me was unsure if I would be alive the next day.

It was hard to sleep that night. I was really cold even under the heavy quilt blanket and full flannel pajamas. I attributed my restlessness to the lack of bed frame beneath the mattress I had pulled into the loft area that Leah and I were sharing. Looking back I see how the night stretched into me and planted the seed of what was to come. Though hidden to me at the time, the dynamic balance of opposites offered by the I-Ching was something that was indeed ahead of me. And I would indeed be turning back.

The life asymmetric was my divination.

CHAPTER 23

SWEET POTATOES

Growing up my parents always hosted Thanksgiving. It was a somewhat traditional meal with the good old standards like cranberries straight from a can and sweet potatoes with marshmallows on top. Where things went off from the norm was that nobody in my family liked mashed potatoes, so we blended traditions and had instead a Jewish celebration food, noodle kugel. Also, in place of pie for dessert, there was a store bought chocolate cake to celebrate my mom's birthday.

During the past decade, Thanksgiving dinners had become more like The Last Supper than celebrations of life and divine goodness. While for most people, the holiday is a time to appreciate their bounty, to assess and praise life's riches, no matter how big or small, for me it had become an event marked by what was about to be lost.

It started in 1997, gathered at Mitchel's Aunt Debbie's house in West Nyack, New York. My mom had flown out East from California to join us, and my sister and her sons, Dylan and Elliott, made the drive from upstate New York. Everyone was rallying together to give Mitchel and me a special Thanksgiving with our two families together. Also at the table were Aunt Debbie's husband and kids and my sister-in-law Jill and her family. Mitchel's mom, Marcia, sat in her wheelchair at one head of the table, her disease leaving only a zombie-like version of herself—eyes vacant, face drawn, and completely disengaged from anything happening around the table.

The second Thanksgiving of Depression was four years later, just after Mitchel and I moved back to California from graduate school in New Jersey and my mom was close to her final hour. I had felt guilty that I didn't even cook her a real turkey for her last Thanksgiving.

But the best part of reflections like these is that they can help us do things another way the next time. Things would be different for Lisa's last Thanksgiving—she was going out with a turkey and all the fixings. I would go back to Rochester to make sure that Lisa's final Thanksgiving was as joyous as possible.

Lisa was declining quickly. With Dylan off at Cornell for his first year of college, it was a lot of pressure on Elliott who was still in high school and home alone with Lisa. One goal of the trip was to set up some home nursing care so that it wouldn't all fall to Elliott.

When my plane touched down in Rochester, a text on my phone from Dylan said that Lisa was in the hospital after another dizzy spell, so he would come to pick me up and take me to her. Arriving at the hospital, Lisa's room was already crowded with people – several of her friends, Bruce, the boys, Joel, and a few hospital staff. I could tell by one look that she was agitated.

"They say I need a plan before I can go home," Lisa said to me without her usually warm hello and hug, as I came into the room.

Joel jumped in to clarify. "They are ready to let her go home, but Dr. Quilt, her palliative care doctor, would like a plan in place for who will care for Lisa when she is home. Everyone is here to talk about next steps."

"I don't want a nurse," Lisa said. "Maybe everyone can take turns checking in on me." I looked around the room at the group of people gathered, everyone looking down at their laps. They had all already done so much. I felt guilty that I lived so far away and couldn't be the one to take over care of my sister. The silence in the room was broken with Joel saying he could take the quarter off teaching and help out, but could not take care of her full time. It was painfully real as each of Lisa's friends took a turn to say, that as much as they loved her, this was just too much for them to take on. Nobody wanted to say it, but it was clear—they were all tapped out. Lisa was disappointed, though I know she understood.

"We'll figure it out, Lis," I said. "For now, let's just get the number for the nursing service so we can get you out of here." I walked out of the room and headed for the nursing station and requested that I get a chance to talk with Dr. Quilt. The man who came to meet me was a huge surprise—his demeanor was almost joyous, not like someone who hung out with dying people all day.

"I'm planning to do a bilateral mastectomy and reconstruction," I told him. "Right now it's scheduled for December. Do you think that's bad timing considering I really want to be here if Lisa needs me?" I felt like I already knew the answer, so I wasn't surprised to hear his yes, but what came next was more of a shocker.

"I'm suggesting you set up home hospice care," he said, using the dreaded "H" word. "She isn't going to make it long enough for you to have the surgery and recover enough to travel back here."

As much as I hated that this was where we had come to—I was thankful that I was there to transition Lisa to her new set-up. But first, we would have a festive celebration, and I didn't have to do a thing to make it happen. An entire meal was brought to my sister's house in several recycled cardboard boxes by Wendy, Bea, and Grace Wickstrom. Last Thanksgiving, Dylan, a junior in high school, was dating Bea Wickstrom, a senior. But when Bea went off to Northwestern the next year, Dylan continued to visit the Wickstrom's, only that time it was little sister Grace who was his gal. But none of that mattered today. This gesture to bring us Thanksgiving dinner was full of love and deep generosity. They knew the sadness of the occasion for our family, and they didn't want our day to be spoiled by hours toiling over a turkey.

Wafts of autumn scents filled the room as the Wickstrom ladies walked into Lisa's house. In Wendy's hands was a box packed with white linens and cloth napkins and a candelabra made of fruit. Bea had a fully cooked turkey in her arms and Grace carried a casserole dish and several platefuls of sides. They also included several additional flourishes, like a beautiful flower display and pre-printed calligraphy name cards. All three women came dressed in their Sunday best, a stark contrast to those of us sitting on Lisa's couches in our jeans and sweaters. But this was all we could do at the time, and everyone understood that.

It would be my first Thanksgiving without Mitchel since we'd met, and of course, my first without my children. Even the cheery narration of the Thanksgiving Day Parade coming from the TV nobody was watching could not break the spell of sadness in the house. Mostly we were trying to think about how best to get through this day—to stay present to the significance of the moment, and at the same time not drown in the sorrow of what was happening.

When the Wickstroms went home for their own Thanksgiving dinner, everyone moved into the dining room and made the requisite comments on how beautiful everything looked. With several courses ahead, nobody dared to admit that the mere thought of eating was repulsive. Everyone looked at me to begin the meal with a grace or blessing. I didn't want to take it on. "This is Lisa's moment," I said. "She's the reason we're gathered here. I think she should start us off."

A silence filled the small room. Nobody dared disagree or even take a breath, looking down in awkwardness so as not to meet Lisa's eyes as she began.

"Well, this is it," she started. "Thanks for all being here. Thanks, Raych, for making the trip."

I glanced at her briefly to acknowledge her appreciation, cocking my head to the side so she wouldn't see the tears running down the other side of my face.

"Of course," I whispered to her, preparing myself for what would come next.

"Let's see what kind of soup they brought," Lisa said.

There was a collective gasp from the table, a reflection of the relief we all were feeling that we had gotten through that painful and awkward moment, as well the stifling of a laugh that this was all she would say. Her big moment, to reflect on life and death, and Lisa decides to skip it and move on to soup. We didn't even raise our glasses.

I felt let down, like somehow there should be more, some larger acknowledgement of what was happening here. If this were the movie "One True Thing" and Lisa were playing Meryl Streep, she would sit proudly, her bald head covered in a purple turban, addressing her family with a voice weak from chemo and exhaustion, and would say something momentous. Or, taking the roll of her daughter, as played by Renee Zellweger, I would stand up at the table and recite all the accomplishments and proud moments of Lisa's life.

But this was real life, and the most profound thing at the table was the fact that next year, Lisa would not be. There were no words for that.

Disneyland, CA. December 25, 2008

CHAPTER 24

PILLOWS

We knew it was coming. Mitchel and I decided to stay somewhat local for winter break, knowing that our trip might be interrupted. Instead of our annual winter in the tropics, Mitchel, the girls, and I headed for our first family trip to Disneyland, hoping two things would come true: first, that by going to the park on Christmas Day we would avoid long lines, and second, that somehow amidst the vividly bright happy setting, I could hide from the doom of my sister's pending death.

Lisa had moved from her home, where she had hoped to stay until her death, to a Hospice House. Her At-Home hospice nurses had called me a few days before when it became clear that any benefits to her mental well being and comfort by being at home were outweighed by the lack of safety staying there. The nurse on duty reported that Lisa was trying to climb on all fours up the stairs toward her bedroom even after weeks of being confined to the lower floor of her house. She believed the hired nurses were jailors, punishing her by not allowing her to move, and tried to go out her front door, in a nightgown, when there were typical Rochester sub-zero temperatures outside.

An ambulance trip to the hospice hospital was her final ride.

In the four days since she had arrived at the hospice house, the workers there noticed a steady decline in her respiration and temperature, suggesting the end was drawing closer. She also hadn't muttered a word since leaving her house.

Joel called the day after we visited Disneyland with the dreaded news—it was time to be at my sister's side. Everything from that point forward blurred. I didn't want to accept what it meant. I didn't want to process the fact that my sister was dying. I went into autopilot.

Mitchel and I and the girls drove a few hours north of LA stopping at an Embassy Suites for a decent night's rest. Sitting in the makeshift office space at the hotel, I used their Wi-Fi to buy myself a plane ticket out of Sacramento the next evening. I didn't try to find the cheapest flight or the best layover spot. I just needed to get there. Trying to decide what day I should book the return trip was devastating. How could I settle on how many days I needed between now, having my sister die, making all the arrangements for her burial and funeral, spending time with family and friends there, and getting her home to be buried next to my parents. I couldn't stand to think about any of it. I decided on a week. I would come back in time to have my kids get back to school after New Year's. A new year without my sister.

On the couch in our suite that night, we told the girls what was happening. Auntie Lisa was dying and mommy needed to go there to say good-bye to her from us. I looked at their little drooping faces that Lisa would never see again. She had named Ruby and had flown cross country within hours of both girls' births to be with me. All I could hope was that they would both hold memories of Lisa after she was gone.

The next morning I couldn't stomach the hotel buffet, I just wanted to get moving and hightail it home so that I could shower, unpack, repack and take a red eye to New York.

Later that night, on the drive to the airport, I took a sleeping pill in hopes of being knocked out before we even took off. Unfortunately it didn't take hold quick enough and I was forced into small talk with my seatmate.

"Is Rochester your final destination," the woman at the window asked.

"Yes," I said, looking down at my backpack, pushing it with my feet under the seat in front of me, knowing that any eye contact would unleash a torrent of tears that I didn't want to release with a stranger. Not seeming to catch on to my non-verbal cues she kept the questions coming.

"Is this a vacation, or work, or are you going home?"

"None of those," I said, wanting to keep things right there. That was all I needed to say. Let her think I am rude. Or lie. But the floodgates were opened and I was already crying.

"My sister lives there. Lived. Well lives. She's dying."

The woman's face sank and then she turned and busied herself with her already fastened seat belt. "I'm so sorry," she muffled, probably now wishing this conversation was over as much as I already did.

I had played out this same routine at least once a year since I was about 14—two flights, usually separated by a layover in Chicago, always hoping that bad weather didn't get in between Lisa and me. Arriving in Ro-cha-cha felt like a second home to me. I knew how to get to Wegman's for groceries and the JCC for a workout, where my favorite movie theater was, and I even had a favorite store, Archiamage on Monroe Avenue. As soon as the plane touched down I would pick up my pace, knowing that I was moments away from seeing Lisa's face.

But not this time. My walk up the terminal was deliberately slow. I even stopped to use the restroom before taking the escalator toward baggage. While waiting for my things I sent a text to Bruce to let him know that I had landed. "I'm on my way," he replied, and I knew he hadn't even left yet.

Bruce pulled up at the airport in Lisa's green Subaru, the trunk, as always, so full of random junk that I had to stuff my baggage in the back seat. Some things never change. But being picked up by Bruce was definitely new; I don't think he had been a part of any of my airport arrivals over the years since before they got divorced while I was still in high school.

There was not much to talk about during the ride. Bruce asked the requisite, "How was your trip?" and I commented on the bitter cold and how unprepared my California blood was for the Rochester winters—this December 27th being no exception.

As we made small talk on the drive, I knew this was the beginning of a new relationship I would need to have with him. He would now be the main connection for me to my nephews.

"I want you to know that Elliott decided to play in his basketball game," Bruce said. "We talked about it this morning, and he knows this is her last day. But I think it will be easier for him this way."

Bruce was right. Elliott had always been the sensitive one in the family. He was the baby who grew up his whole life under the shadow of Lisa's cancer. He didn't need to watch her die, too.

Out the car window, large dirty snow banks lined the freeway. While I was familiar with the directions from the airport to Lisa's house, this was an unfamiliar trip.

The entry to the Hildebrandt Hospice House looked like so many hospital spaces I had seen before, with an element of elegant residence thrown in. Pale tans and gentle blue walls, colors meant to soothe, and the lights dimmed to an easy-on-the-eye level that allowed the crying and short on sleep eyes of visitors enough cover. Peering into a few rooms as we moved down the hall I could see that the furnishings and art on the walls were completely generic save for a few ironic "Get Well" cards sitting on window sills from well wishers who just didn't get it. In some rooms, well-placed bouquets of flowers desperately tried to draw attention away from the person in the bed.

Bruce stopped in front of a closed door and pushed it open. As I walked through the doorway I froze. I don't know what I was expecting to see but not a lump on the bed. Lisa's body, covered by the sheets, jerked at uneven intervals as she worked overtime to take breaths, like a fish out of water. Her bald head looked tiny peeking out of the covers. Nobody had bothered with her wig for a few weeks now. I wished it were there and I could give it to her. *She would have wanted to die with hair on her head*, I thought to myself, wondering if I was the only one who would know this about her.

As I walked up to Lisa's bed, Dylan got up and gave me a huge hug.

Making my way around to the other side, Joel got up and gave me a hug and offered me the chair he'd been sitting on next to Lisa's head.

When I got closer I could see that her face was strained, squeezed up like she had just tasted a lime. Joel told me that she looked more at ease after I got there and I could tell that she felt my presence.

I took her hand in mine. It was cold from a lack of circulation. Still, I held on tight, thinking that by holding her hand I could keep Lisa tethered to the earth and she wouldn't die. We took turns shifting who sat at Lisa's head to whisper in her ear. I only left once for a few minutes, to use the restroom and get some tea, and to allow Dylan space to say his good-byes to his mom. When I came back in the room I caught him stroking her head in a tender way only a son could do to his dying mom. Without a word, Dylan got up, gently kissed Lisa's forehead and left me alone in the room.

I crawled up into the bed, lying on my side on the sliver of space left next to her. My feet dug their way down the covers, finding hers for a last bit of footsie. Crying on her shoulder, I went through old stories trying to find one last laugh to have together. Although she could no longer speak, Lisa communicated with me through her breath—showing me her fear, her regrets and her triumphs in grunts. Her pale blue eyes, though glazed, peered at me with deep love.

I reviewed her work life– social services, youth leadership, special needs adults, Red Cross. She had made a huge impact on so many people. I promised to follow through on my breast surgery and face my genetic fate of cancer. She had helped me save myself and create a different life for my family. This was our final gift to each other.

I whispered affirmations in her ear:

> I love you Lisa.
> I love you.
> You have been a most excellent sister.
> You have raised two amazing human beings, who also love you so much.
> My children love you.
> You are a loyal and generous friend and person.
> You will always be a star in my sky and your love will live on.

I had practiced these words on the airplane. I knew from helping my mom die how important it was that Lisa hear these things. They would help her let go.

A single tear curled up in the corner of her eye, slowly, and just sat there, an acknowledgment that she heard me, until it dried away and her eyes dropped closed for the last time. After a few minutes I got out of bed and walked out to the hallway to gather Bruce, Dylan and Joel. We gathered around her bed, everyone touching Lisa as her breathing slowed. Holding Lisa's hand I could still feel it pulsing, as I whispered the lyrics to "Blackbird" by the Beatles: "Take these broken wings and learn to fly." While I was releasing Lisa, she was doing the same for me, giving me flight and hope for a different future.

Three hours after I landed on the East Coast to say good-bye, my sister died.

That night, returning to Lisa's house without her, I put one of her rings on my middle right finger, tying us together through this bloodline forever. It was a spiral shape fitted with five small stones. I made up a story that each gem was a member of my family, once five, and now reduced to two. I would wear it every day thereafter to support and comfort me with her love through all the trials that were about to unfold.

CHAPTER 25

FOG LIGHTS

The last day of 2009 easily made my list of the top three worst days of my life.

While most people were making lists of how they would improve themselves in the year ahead, I was barreling through my own inventory—all the things I needed to do to prepare for my sister's burial and service. On my list: meet with the funeral director to decide the type of burial and what clothes my sister would wear in her casket, pick materials for her shroud and casket, and order transportation for her body to and from the service, and then later across the country. We also had to order food for all the visitors who would come back to Lisa's house for the Jewish custom of *shiva*, where the family in mourning sits at home for a few days to receive well wishers honoring the deceased and the family. Even in death you can't host a Jewish event without food. *Shiva* also meant cleaning the house. It seemed strange to have to do all these menial tasks while in the very first day of mourning, but it did help pass the time and avoid the draw of dark thoughts I couldn't handle at the moment.

There was also the task of writing Lisa's obituary. With my mom and dad's deaths, Lisa had helped me with the details. She had an uncanny ability to remember certain stories of how and when people met, and how they were all related, that made her a better family storyteller than I ever will be. She could name all the 4th cousins, once removed, while I couldn't remember the 1st cousins alone. I conferred with Joel and Bruce to be sure I got Lisa's birthplace and year, college dates and degrees, and marriage and family details in proper order.

The last and most challenging task was to write Lisa's eulogy. I was so tired of having to write these public good-bye speeches. It felt like someone else's turn. I knew I would start with a story I heard told once about the dash that comes between the birth and death dates on a gravestone. It is in this dash, the story tells us, that life is lived. Perhaps this was a cheesy place to start my speech, but it was true. And Lisa's dash had been big, juicy, and full of great adventures, excellent music, strong relationships, and, unfortunately, too many challenges. But she lived the dash, more than most people I had ever met. Lisa never lived like she was dying.

Lisa was always my best friend, big sister, cool mom and twin separated by 16 years. Some of Lisa's best moments were when people asked which of the two of us was older, and the worst when they asked if she was my mom.

I wanted to share my favorite early memory when Lisa took me to my first concert—Hall and Oates at the Concord Pavilion. The best part of the whole night was eating gigantic chocolate chip cookies, while listening to "Your Kiss is On My List," and laughing so hard we almost rolled down the hill into our fellow concertgoers.

But realizing a eulogy is not meant to be one person's trip down memory lane, I shifted the focus to Lisa and the qualities she left within each of us.

One of the themes of her life that came through loud and clear was her love of everything about music. Lisa's life was filled with Beatlemania, Grateful Dead concerts, a huge vinyl collection, and a passion for pop culture. She even named her first son after one of her all time favorites, Bob Dylan. Lisa's life had a continual soundtrack – and this was before the invention of the iPod. Music was always more than background to Lisa - it offered healing, inspiration, and light, even on the darkest of days. At one point, completely mesmerized by the musical artist India Arie, Lisa ordered 100 copies of her CD *Testimony* and handed them out to every person she cared about so that they, too, could find inspiration in the rhythms and lyrics. How many people do you know who would buy 100 gifts? That pretty much defines Lisa.

Another quality of Lisa that would shine through to all of us left behind was her incredible penchant for friendship. With Lisa, friendship was not just about time, it was also about loyalty. Some of her best friends she had known for only a few years, but you would never know it. If you walked into Wegman's grocery store with Lisa at any hour of any day, it would take you a minimum of an hour to get out of there. On every aisle there was someone who Lisa knew and liked and she could tell you great details of their life story. Not because she was a *yenta* (gossip), but because she cared about people like that.

The other thing about Lisa was her profound ability to endear herself to the most generous, big hearted, unconditional people you could ever meet. Random individuals came into Lisa's life and offered her unsolicited plane trips, basement makeovers, foot rubs, groceries, trips to concerts or Broadway shows, and so much more. Perhaps my eulogy could properly thank all those people. And she gave all this back, and then some, with her love.

Of all these great qualities, Lisa's strongest suit was her laughter. She had a full bellied, powerful, whole body laugh. Mitchel even named some of her laughs based on their style: "slappies" for when Lisa slapped her legs, and "stompy town" when she would bang her feet on the floor, all the while gasping for breath. I believe that for Lisa, laughter was healing, a way to vent, let off steam, and engage in life in a deep and meaningful way.

But the ultimate way that Lisa touched this world was in the way she raised and loved her two sons, Dylan and Elliott. Lisa worked very hard at being a mom – and not necessarily in the traditional domestic ways of cooking and cleaning. Lisa parented by teaching them to be good people: to be thoughtful, curious, and passionate. She always listened to the boys, and not just waiting to reply, but to really hear their words. She was interested in who they were becoming as people, even if it was different than her own experience.

I love to tell the story of when Lisa talked with the boys about feminism when they were just 11 and 8 years old. An Eminem song had just come on the car radio, and Lisa quickly changed the channel, but then both boys said they liked that song and asked her to put it back on. Lisa, aware that Eminem's lyrics were less than flattering toward women, decided it was time for them to learn about misogyny. A lively discussion ensued, with Lisa stressing that as a card-carrying member of NOW she felt it was important that they know this, and then they could make a decision about whether or not they still wanted to listen to his music. And when they chose to keep the tracks rolling, Lisa never passed judgment on their choice, appreciating that they were becoming music connoisseurs.

Given everything Lisa was battling with over the years – the only thing I ever heard her express worry about was what would happen to the boys after she was gone, and her biggest sorrow was that she would not get a chance to be a part of key times in their lives like graduations, weddings, and hopefully the birth of their own children. I know Lisa found great comfort in knowing that Bruce was a good father to the boys, that they were surrounded by great community and friends, and that Joel, Mitchel and I would walk to the end of the earth for those two.

And of course Lisa gave me the great gift of life. While it pained her that BRCA was another trait we shared, she was also unconditionally happy for me that I could walk a different path. My words would thank her for helping me have the title of Previvor.

To end my eulogy I needed to quote one of her favorite songs, so I picked "Unwritten," by Natasha Bedingfield.

> *Drench yourself in words unspoken*
> *Live your life with arms wide open*
> *Today is where your book begins*
> *The rest is still unwritten*

My eulogy written, and the funeral preparations finished, all I could do was wait for the year to end. Dylan, Elliott, Joel, Bruce and I went to a BBQ joint for the New Year's Eve dinner. We tried to be somewhat festive and everyone ordered a beer but I guessed everyone was only hoping to drown out a little bit of the pain and emptiness. Getting home before midnight on the east coast meant I could call my family out west and be able to have New Year's with Mitchel and the girls. We blew New Year's horns across the phone lines, hoping for better blessings to be bestowed on our family in the year ahead. Then I spent the first hour of the New Year getting ready for my sister's funeral before tucking myself to sleep in her bed, surrounded by all the cherished things that made up her life.

I hoped for sleep to come easily and for my dreams to wash away the thought that all the year ahead of me had to offer was a funeral and burial.

CHAPTER 26

ZEPPELINS

I slipped out of Lisa's house in the middle of the night—another in a life-long string of avoiding good-byes. Nobody heard me leave and I drove myself to the airport where I boarded a plane, along with my sister's body, so we could bury her at home in California.

We buried Lisa to the right of my mom so they lay side by side. My dad's grave was just under Lisa's toes. They were quite the triumvirate lying there six feet under. I couldn't stand to see them all reduced to grass rectangles. Only my mom and dad's graves had headstones since my sister's grave would remain unmarked, as is the Jewish custom, until the one-year anniversary/*yortzeit* of her passing. It was thought that the year between the burial and gravestone unveiling rituals measured the proper time necessary to mourn.

But my mourning period was truncated. Unlike the physical preparation I made to train for the half marathon before my original surgery date, my preparation was more of an emotional and logistical epic. There wasn't much time to lose if I were to have the surgery before my 36th birthday, the age Lisa was when she was first diagnosed with cancer. I had promised Lisa that I would do the surgery as she took her final breaths.

My main priority was to get things lined up for my girls, so that life, with all its shuffling, carrying, and errands, could continue as normally as possible while I was in the hospital and then home healing. We asked our family friends, Lee and Jackie, to step in as surrogate parents and move their family of three girls to our house for a few days while we were in San Francisco. It was a big job requiring that all five kids spanning in ages from 2 to 14 get to their perspective schools. Plus there would be extra, very finicky, mouths to feed, and the shuffling of adults and kids to various activities, workplaces, and appointments. Nonetheless, Lee and Jackie said yes without missing a beat.

In prepping for my recovery, I created an account on helpinghands.com, a free website that allows the user to coordinate activities and manage volunteers amongst their community. I could post a need for anything from a ride to an appointment to help with laundry. As I gathered up names of all my contacts I could hear Hillary Clinton in my head saying, "It takes a village," and this was just the place to gather my troops. I tested the system on March 17th, a week before my surgery, with a post letting everyone know where and when the surgery was taking place, keeping the tone light and somewhat silly by mentioning how excited I was about the Peet's coffee cart in the lobby. Within an hour there were already comments and good wishes on my lots of helping hands website wall, but one stood out among the rest. It was from Beth Jaeger-Skien, a woman I'd worked with 12 years earlier, and hadn't heard from since. She saw my Helping Hands post that I linked to Facebook and got in touch immediately. She was BRCA+ as well and on her second day home after having the same surgery at the same hospital that I would be going to soon.

I picked up the phone immediately and called Beth. It had been so long it was hard to know where to start. We were both moms to girls now. Beth's twin girls were about the same age as Marley. She told me her breast cancer family history and I shared mine. She sounded winded on the phone, but then again I hadn't talked to her in so long it was hard to know if that was her usual sound or a symptom of the surgery. It was exciting and comforting to talk with her. She was the first person I really knew that had a DIEP surgery, and so recently that she would remember details to share with me that others had left off. We decided to meet in person two days later when I went in for my pre-op visit.

The visit with my surgeon was uneventful given what was ahead of me. His physician assistant, Mary, ran me through the regular routine of weight, blood pressure, and temperature before Dr. King whisked into the room, showed me his big blue eyes, and spent about five minutes going over what to expect with the surgery and recovery.

The procedure would take eight hours. He would be with me the whole time, even during the mastectomy, assisting the breast surgeon for that part before beginning the reconstruction. I would wake up in the ICU so that they could monitor me for the first twenty-four hours.

Dr. King talked briefly about the medications they would give me: antibiotics as well as pain medication would be flowing even before I was rolled into the OR. Dr. King extended his arm to shake my hand. "You're going to do great," he said, and then he was gone.

On my way to Beth's house I grabbed one of my favorite SF foods, a grilled falafel from Truly Mediterranean. I also tucked into a cute bath store to get lavender products, a candle, and some scar balm that I put together as a healing kit for Beth. When I rang the doorbell, Beth's husband answered and brought me to the living room before excusing himself to get her from the kitchen. When she appeared on his arm, her body looked tight, her shoulders stiff and she had a grimace on her face. She walked slowly and deliberately, like she didn't want any more movement than necessary. It was unclear if it was the time that had passed since last seeing her, or the effects of the surgery, but Beth looked much older than I remembered.

At one point Beth's daughter, Zoe, came to where she was sitting on the couch and asked if she could cuddle. "Not now sweet pea," Beth said, "you know Mommy can't have you leaning on her right now." My heart dropped to think of my little girls feeling displaced by my surgery. I remember having a similar issue with Marley, when I was pregnant with Ruby, and "her lappy" was taken over by my big belly.

I tried not to be frightened by what I was seeing in Beth and instead focused on the stories she told of her days before surgery and how well she was treated in the hospital. She shared with me a terrific idea for a ritual to do with my kids before surgery—visit a Build-A-Bear store and have a kid-friendly conversation about what was about to happen to me.

Beth and I kept the conversation light and short. We both knew there was so much more to say but also that this was not the time. As I walked out the door of her flat, Beth called out, "One week and it's your turn," and gave me a great smile and farewell wave. I could tell she was attempting to sound optimistic, but her comment left me filled with dread. As I drove back to Davis that evening, my emotions were conflicted; feeling like my surgery was on one hand, no big deal, and on the other, the biggest deal of all.

When I got home and shared my experience with Mitchel, what resonated for us both was the idea of taking the girls to Build-A-Bear. It seemed like a grand idea to surround ourselves with hundreds of fluffy, happy, stuffed animals as we told the girls about what was coming. Our plan was to go to the store only a few days before my surgery so that they wouldn't have to spend too long worrying about what was going to happen, but also giving them long enough that they could process it before saying good-bye.

Walking into the store, I picked up the shell of a stuffed monkey from where it hung waiting to be chosen by some adoring child. "Girls, see how this monkey needs to get some filling?"

"Yes, Mama," Marley said, barely looking up from the bins of stuffed animal shells she was perusing. Ruby didn't say anything, but grabbed the unfilled monkey from my hands. I wasn't sure she was going to get any of this. *How could a two year old possibly understand that her mommy was going to the hospital to have her breasts removed so that she could live a healthier life*, I thought to myself, but kept on explaining anyway.

"Next week, when I have my surgery, it's going to be like this. Mama needs to get some fresh stuffing just like this monkey. See how it has a little cut right there? That's so they can put the stuffing in and then sew it back up."

My breasts had provided sustenance for the first few years of their lives. They had no knowledge of what this all was about or could mean. Their sweet little faces peered up at me like they understood, but I could tell they were more excited to go back to the bins of fuzzy creatures all over the place. I took solace in the fact that they seemed perfectly distracted by the idea of picking their creature to stuff, and decided to end the conversation there.

Both girls picked teddy bears, Ruby's bright pink bear covered with white hearts and Marley's a classic brown bear. I made a short recording to tuck inside the bears palms so that the girls could hear my voice say, "Hi Ruby/Marley, this is mommy and daddy. We love you soooo much. Forever and always. Kisses and hugs."

"Every time you think of us you can just push the button and we're right there with you," Mitchel said. Dreadfully, my brain drifted to thinking of the possibility of dying in surgery, of leaving these two girls and the man whom I loved to do life without me.

Snapping back to myself, I brought our newly stuffed creatures to the checkout counter. Though we tried to pull it off as educational, I think the trip and the bears were a consolation prize for what they were about to give up ahead. Our stuffing ritual ended with 67 dollars worth of bribery, comfort and hope.

The night I said my final goodbye to the girls before I went to the hospital, it all seemed worth it when each of my daughters had her new stuffy next to her pillow. It was both beautiful and tragic to look at them like that, tucked into the sheets with a stuffed animal that would be their surrogate mommy for a little while.

CHAPTER 27

SACRIFICIAL OFFERINGS

Packing my suitcase for a two to four day stay at a hospital where my breasts would be cut off and reformed was not an easy task. I would wear a bra to the hospital but would not need one on the way home, so just underwear went into the bag. I brought two sets of pajamas—an organic cotton tee shirt with shorts and one warm fleece set. I had been told to go for satin or silk for the smoothest surface against my skin. I also brought a pair of slippers and several pairs of socks since I'd been warned that I would always want my feet covered in the hospital.

Although I had never been a patient in a hospital before, I could imagine that I would want to get out of the hospital gown as soon as possible. I was also clear that I would want loose and comfortable, so I packed several yoga pants and t-shirts. All the resources on breast reconstruction suggest bringing layers so you can go braless and not have to feel exposed. Hospitals are notorious for either being too hot or excessively cold so I threw in a zip-up hoodie (the zipper would prove crucial) and two scarves for good measure. The only item I bought specifically for this was a marathon bib belt that I got because my friend Cath said it was a lifesaver after her surgery. She used it to hold all the drains in place around her waist.

In the side pocket of my duffle I put my favorite book, *Temple of My Familiar*, a journal and my IPod Nano, which I had loaded with all my favorite tunes for feeling upbeat and chilling out. I made sure to bring my pillow so that I could have comfort from home in the hospital and because I'd heard it really helped to put a pillow between your chest and the seat belt on the drive home. Last, but certainly not least, a few too many photos of my daughters. Saying good-bye to Marley and Ruby had been the hardest moment of the whole process. Mitchel and I waited until bedtime to leave so I could read a story and tuck them in one more time. We would spend the night in a friend's condo in San Francisco so we would be ready bright and early to head to the hospital.

When it was time to say goodnight I tried not to overrun the girls with kisses and hugs for fear it would freak them out, but I wanted them for me. I had never been away from the girls for this long before, and we weren't sure yet if they would come visit me for my birthday four days later or if I would already be home, so I didn't know when our next hug would be. Holding back the tears, saving them for the car ride to the city, I left them under the covers, their Build-A-Bear stuffies guarding over them, promising that everything was going to be all-right.

That night Mitchel and I attempted to watch a movie although for the life of me I don't think I could recall what that movie was. It was irrelevant; my eye already on what was coming tomorrow. *Take a shower*, I thought to myself. *Go feel how the water runs off your breasts.*

It was a nice idea, but the whole time I was in the shower all I could think about was that I had absolutely no way to hold onto any of the sensations I could feel in my chest. Maybe I would have that experience that some amputees have where they feel a ghost limb. All I knew was it would never feel exactly the same again.

In the shower, I noted how the water ran off my breasts, creating a waterfall from my chest to my toes. I closed my eyes and enjoyed the feeling of running the soap all over my body.

As I dried off after, I noticed that as my body cooled, my nipples hardened and protruded from my blouse. I felt all these things – but it was impossible to appreciate them except in an intellectual way, thinking to myself, this will feel different, but not having any sensibility about what that different would be like.

I made mental notes on how it felt to unlatch my bra behind my back. I certainly wouldn't be wearing a proper bra for a long time. A lot of books suggested purchasing bras that latch in the front post-mastectomy. Since I was a teenager with barely a cupful of breast, I always really enjoyed the feeling of taking off my bra at the end of the day. I never really noticed it much until that moment where I released the strap and ah! It's one of those sweet moments in the day when everything is done, the kids are fast asleep, and I can really relax.

There were other post-surgery concerns I had read about, but one that stuck out from the rest was that for many women, sexual desire and self-esteem were diminished after mastectomy. While I continued to hold hope that I would fly through surgery and come out of all this with a hot new mom bod, there was no way to know how it would all feel. No matter what happened, mine wouldn't be the body I has known for the past 36 years.

Lying face down in the bed, I took note of the coolness of the taupe colored sheets and lamented that this was a position I would miss for a while. Flipping over, I scanned my chest to see it one last time this way, my ice cream scoop mounds looking as if they were slowly melting and sliding toward my armpit from the power of gravity and years of breastfeeding. I watched my breasts rise and fall as I took deep breaths, wondering if the new tissue would react in this same way. Tears rolled down my cheeks and left a soft puddle on my pillowcase when Mitchel walked into the room.

"Lay with me," I said. "I just want to feel what my body feels like against yours."

Not yet washed up or in his pajamas, Mitchel sensed my urgency and climbed into bed. Spooning my body against his, I felt my breasts press into his back. His neck smelled of a mixture of shampoo and cologne. He wasn't a usual cologne wearer, but we had gone out for a special dinner, a last supper of sorts, and for Mitchel, cologne went along with getting dressed up.

I wriggled my body free of our spoon and turned his body toward mine. I wanted to be chest to chest. Mitchel took off his shirt and I could feel the warmth of our hearts meeting. I tried my best to imprint these feelings, to catalog them as sensations I would be able to come back and retrieve some day.

Slowly we both peeled off our clothes. I had assumed we would do it that night since we didn't have kids to worry about, and besides, it seemed almost ritualistic—the glory before the sacrifice. It would likely be weeks before we had sex again, so it felt like the least I could do for this man that was about to sit by and support me, as I was pulled apart and rebuilt. He had loved my body since I was 22 years old, when my breasts were still athletic and perky and tan. Together we created the babes that had nursed for years from my bosom. They had been his cupful and he was probably having his own feelings about what was next.

The actual sex was a bit lackluster for me. It was hard to get my libido super psyched when all I could think about was being naked on the operating table the next morning. I tried to focus in on the details of the present—the smoothness of my belly without scars, the way my breasts got warm and warmer the closer I came to climax, the flush of red across my entire chest that would stay for a good fifteen minutes after I had an orgasm.

It would probably never feel like this again. Most women I had spoken to said they lost most, if not all, sensation in the chest area after reconstruction. Some people said their skin felt prickly or otherwise different. Slowly these thoughts started seeping in and taking me away from my body and the experience. As much as I tried to pull myself back, all I could think about was the next day, already envisioning myself in a hospital gown being pushed on a gurney.

Desperate to be in my body, with my husband, I shook these thoughts away and enjoyed our union. I tried to take notes in my mind about the sensations I was feeling of body on body, my body, whole, unmarred. When we were done, I had my final sips of water, and tried to fall asleep. Sounds of soft jazz came from the condo walls- so familiar after my first 18 years of life listening with my mom to her favorite radio station, KBLX, the Quiet Storm. The comfort of this memory, mixed with the music and Mitchel's warm body close to mine lulled me toward sleep.

I felt nervous, yet ready. While it was my first time having a surgery and going under, the end point was something I had known I wanted for some time. My presurgery outlook was positive: I'm young, healthy, and strong. I will snap back, and when I do, it will be into my new sexy shape. This was my chance for a life in asymmetry from my mom and sister.

Even my dreams did not indicate that I would deviate from my plan. I didn't see the nightmare ahead. Yet later I'd separate my life between how it was before the surgery and how it would be forever after.

CHAPTER 28

FLAPS

The combo of little sleep, not being allowed my morning coffee, and the fear of what was ahead made the car ride full of dread. Mitchel tried to make light of the tension by chatting about the places we were passing and their significance to our relationship: Market Street, where we'd seen our first concert together, Golden Gate and Divisidero, the Western Addition, where I lived when Mitchel and I first met; the Lower Height, where we'd enjoyed many a brunch. Unfortunately reminiscing about those days had the reverse effect, and instead of helping me calm and focus, it made me think of better times when my mom, pop and sister were alive. It was so hard to be doing this without all of them. It didn't seem right that the people who most cared about my outcome were not there to bear witness to my choice. I thought of Mitchel getting married months after his mom died and how my mom never knew any of my children.

I was glad when we arrived in the parking lot of the hospital and these thoughts were pushed out of my mind. I walked as slowly as possible, my pillow slung under my arm, Mitchel's hand in mine, aware this might be the last fresh air I would breath for a while and that these were my last moments as a regular person. Thankfully the lobby of the hospital was able to fool me into thinking I was a tourist visiting the foggy city for pleasure. Lovely fabric couches dotted the large open room and the high vaulted ceilings lent themselves perfectly to the floor to roof windows offering golden views of the City by the Bay. There was a Peet's coffee cart—which I mistakenly imagined I would be visiting during my stay, a gift shop—that I would also never peruse, and a large bank of elevators. It was as much hotel as hospital.

The only indication that I was not on a get-away weekend was the check-in area, with two chairs, a modest desk, file folders and pamphlets marking it clearly as more medical than spa. To put it in ink, after confirming my birthday and social security number to my "host," I was given a plastic bracelet that did not grant me access to the pool and waterslides but rather a gurney ride to the OR.

After "checking in," Michel and I were greeted by a young man in a burgundy suit with a yellow hospital crest button on his lapel.

"F-F-Follow me," he said, and led us to a bank of elevators and then up to the admitting area. "I'm Don, your admitting nurse. Here is a r-r-robe for you. Open in the back. Put all your personal items in this b-b-bag," Don said as he handed me a plastic bag with the hospitals name marked in block letters and walked out of the room.

Slowly I took off each piece of clothing, sure that I wouldn't be back to those clothes for some time. I unsnapped my bra, wondering if I would wear this one again with my new breasts. Stuffing all my personal items into a plastic bag I felt like a convict heading into jail.

Clearly I was not at a resort. This was not a spa robe. I was not going on vacation.

After a few minutes, Don returned to my exam room and gestured toward the exam table. "Have a s-s-seat," he said and proceeded to take my medical history. Hearing my voice say the word "cancer" several times, mentioning my Previvor status, talking in the past tense about my mom and my sister—it always took its toll, but this time was even more nerve racking given how Don's stutter belabored the whole process. I teetered between feeling annoyed with how long this was taking and like a bad human for being mad about his stutter.

After all the verbal data was collected Don took my blood pressure and temperature and confirmed that I was there for a mastectomy and DIEP flap reconstruction. I thought we were done when he handed me the pile of warm blankets, socks and a blue surgical cap.

But then Don said, "Just j-j-jump down from the table for a sec and let me get your weight."

I hated taking my weight, and especially in front of Mitchel. He would always generously look away, but the fear of him turning and seeing the number on the scale still stressed me out. This was a long held concern dating back to high school when I dated a road cyclist named Gavin who kept himself thin (and with shaven legs) and weighed ten pounds less than me. With Mitchel, equally fit, his weight being under mine had already happened, but I was pregnant. This time however, I was distracted by a different disturbing thought as I looked at the scale—*how many of those pounds would be lost instantly when they remove my breasts?*

Don's voice interrupted these somewhat disturbing thoughts. "I'll call a g-g-gurney to get you. G-g-good luck with everything."

Within a few minutes my ride arrived along with a new cast in the hospital staff circus— a strapping young man with dreadlocks and emerald eyes. "Let's roll," he said, pointing to the gurney outside the door. I imagined he used that line several times a day.

"Okay if I come with you?" Mitchel asked.

"Of course," he replied. I half expected him to break into a Jamaican accent. *Of course mahn. Don't you worry about nothing. Jah will provide.*

My Rasta nurse rolled me into the elevator and tried to situate the gurney so that Mitchel could fit in as well. Trying to make conversation and avoid the inevitable awkward elevator silence I stupidly said, "I like your hair," which only made things more uncomfortable. I was sitting up in a gurney, in an open backed hospital gown; with my husband and a guy I would only know for five minutes that probably thought I was making a pass at him.

Relief came quickly as the doors opened and Nurse Dread pulled me over to a desk in the center of the large space to check me in.

"Can you confirm your birthday and social security sweetie?" the dyed blond twenty-something at the nurse's station asked me. Upon successfully identifying myself to the attendant, my chauffeur backed me up, docked me in a holding area, and took off. Mitchel and I spent a few minutes assessing the scene around us—lots of folks in hospital beds and staff running all over the place with medical files and machines.

As I looked toward the far end of the room I caught sight of Dr. King, my surgeon, talking with a nurse. His polo shirt and khakis and dark tan made him look like he was heading out for eight hours on the golf course rather than the operating room. Sauntering up to my hospital bed, and not uttering even a hello, he pulled back my hospital gown and took one final look at my natural breasts. Pulling a purple sharpie from his pants pocket, Dr. King began marking on my body where incisions were to be made. "Like a dry erase board," he joked. He drew a large ellipse across my belly to mark where he would harvest my abdominal tissue and two smaller circles on my chest to mark the center point for the new breasts he would build. The way he slashed the pen at me felt like I was being attacked by a big bully taking advantage of the fact that I was down and couldn't fight back.

"Take a look and let me know if you have any changes," he said.

I looked down at my chest covered in this tattoo of purple hash marks. I had no idea what any of it meant—how could I make suggestions?

"Just make sure they're even," I said.

"I'll see you in there," Dr. King said, and turned to Mitchel to give him a handshake. "The desk staff will give you updates as we have them and will let you know when you can come back to see her in recovery."

"Okay," Mitchel responded, holding Dr. King's hand for a moment too long. I could tell by the forlorn look in his eyes and the way he held the handshake a little too long that he was desperate to make a connection with the guy who was about to hold my life in that very palm.

My next visitor was the Anesthesiologist, who asked me if I had any known allergies to medications.

"My mom was allergic to Penicillin," I said. "But I don't think I have anything."

Making some notes on my paperwork, he then told me about the cocktail he would be giving me that would last for the full 8-10 hour surgery and I made a few jokes about how he was like the drug pusher and asked if I could call him Candy Man.

"I'm going to have my assistant come and set up your IV. Any questions before I see you in there?"

The lab tech looked like he hadn't seen the light of day in a while and didn't offer much hope that he would be able to deal with my testy veins.

"Everyone always has a hard time," I told him on the third or fourth try, not sure why I felt compelled to try to make him feel better. It was my arm after all. After several missed pokes, he finally got a vein he liked.

"How long till I feel that?" I asked, wanting a moment to say my good-byes with Mitchel with a clear head.

"A few minutes probably," he said, "it depends."

I reached for Mitchel's hand with my one arm that wasn't hooked into an IV and looked into his eyes, not sure what to say, but wanting to be in the safety of his eyes. Both of us crying, we exchanged our "love you's" and the next thing I knew my hospital bed was on the move. I'm not sure that there was more to say at that moment anyway, but I remember feeling like I wished I had said something profound, as he became a small speck at the end of the long hallway.

Rolling toward the operating room, I felt like I was in a movie—the endless white tile corridor after corridor, red warning signs and directions covering the walls, large well sealed off doors that opened with the touch of a blue handicap button. Each hallway was progressively colder than the last until we were in the operating room.

Dr. King greeted me first. "Here we go then. You remember Mary, my PA?" he said, and gestured at the woman in a surgical gown standing slightly behind him. "Did you have some music you wanted me to play?" Yes, I said, handing him my iPod with my non-IV bound arm. "It's the Hypnobirthing playlist," I said. I had uploaded a CD of songs set to the sounds of whales that we played every night as we put Marley to sleep as a baby. Countless hours I spent rocking her in my arms or bouncing her on the exercise ball to the sounds of those whales. Beautiful.

A nurse, only identifiable by a poof of orange hair jutting out from her surgical cap and her Sponge Bob Square Pants scrubs, attempted to help me move from bed to operating table. Navigating a surgical gown while on drugs was a challenge. I held on to the back, trying to keep from "mooning" the room and maintain a modicum of modesty, even though I knew it would be taken away in moments. Sure enough, within moments of lying down on the table the nurse asked that I "scoot my bottom up a bit" and all pride vanished.

"My photos," I said, pointing at the gurney they were moving away. I was allowed to bring a few photos of my loved ones into the OR with me. I picked a great family photo of the four of us at our niece Jamie's bat mitzvah and another one of me and my mom and my sister on the cliffs of a beach somewhere when I was about 13 and Lisa was 29. It still felt impossible that they were both gone and crazy to think that Lisa had been my age now when she first got diagnosed with breast cancer. And here I was, about to cut off my breasts in hopes of something different, modeling a new reality for my daughters who I hoped and prayed would have even better options than I had.

I handed the photos over to Nurse Orange who tucked them under my sheets and proceeded to move my arms horizontally into metal holders, like a Jewish Christ, bound to the operating table cross. Perhaps the surgery would be my resurrection, the sweet redemption of a chance to live a new life, free of the fear of breast cancer. *I really am on drugs*, I thought.

A bunch of people began to go to work all around me, covering me with various leads, plugging me into a pulse-ox monitor, and wrapping my free arm in a blood pressure cuff. There was already an IV in the other arm, which they began to fill with the drugs that would deliver amnesia, pain medication and relaxation.

I could sense myself fading, sinking into the background of life, a fog cloud descending on my brain.

A woman's hand was holding an oxygen mask over my face but all I could see were her gold painted nails. *It must be the orange haired nurse*, I thought, *Sponge Bob scrubs and nails with bling!*

"Are you ready?" The anesthetist's voice called toward me from somewhere near my feet. Mustering up the final smidgens of consciousness I had available, I squinted in the distance to see his form. Whatever I had going into my arm must have already been at work because he looked like he was wearing palm tree scrubs and dangling a ziploc bag of weed and saying: "Are you ready?"

With the mask covering my mouth all I could do was nod yes. *Ready as I'll ever be*, I thought.

"Now just take a deep breath," the lady with the golden nails told me and then released the mask. Looking into her face she became a dealer at a poker game.

As I drifted off I remembered small things. Like how funny everyone looked in their masks and surgical caps, or how the air smelled antiseptic, and the tinking sounds of steel utensils being prepped for surgery.

"This is the time to think about a special place you want to go," the anesthesiologist said, luring me toward a peaceful rest.

"I'm walking along the beach— somewhere tropical."

"Watch the surf for a while," a voice said, "and when you wake up it will all be done."

In the next moments I had the sensation of floating in water— all sound, light and sensation muted. Slowly my eyes stopped moving, and I dropped into a deeper consciousness than sleep. My body was completely unprotected, at the mercy of the Candy Man Anesthesiologist and ultimately the masked-man holding a scalpel.

And then I was swimming. Floating with *honus*, the ancient Hawaiian sea turtles named for these creatures that represent the Navigator, filled with the sensation of safety. These were creatures I knew well, and one thing for sure, these creatures could always find their way home. There were enough of them to be my complete family—Ruby, Marley, Mitchel, Joel and Lisa, my parents. They would lead me.

Moving my arms in and out against the water at a perfect 76 degrees.

The sun's rays filtering through the water lighting up the underworld.

I could hold my breath forever.

There was only water, my family honus, and me.

Swimming in the light.

Finding home.

CHAPTER 29

BUMPERS

All around me I heard beeps and bells, a cacophony of murmurs I could not make out, and the sounds of footsteps. But no matter how many times I blinked, I could not bring myself fully into the present. I willed my eyes to open and leave the world of deep slumber I had inhabited for whatever was ahead.

"Hi, Sweetie," I heard Mitchel's voice luring me out from the unconscious. My heavy eyelids opened and shut, letting in tiny waves of light and reality, and then, back to darkness. After a few moments I was able to keep my eyes open long enough to make out his shape next to me. I could see we were holding hands yet I didn't feel the connection. Joel was at the end of the bed standing. Above Mitchel's head I saw a clock and although I couldn't make out the exact time, it was certainly a long way past the 7 am I remembered from the clock in the pre-op area. How strange to have lost time like that.

"Long trip," Joel's voice called out to me as if he could read my mind. Maybe it was my lack of focus but he looked teary-eyed and I realized it was probably hard for him to see me this way. I was married now and a mom, but I would always be the little sister he was watching out for. With both my parents and Lisa gone, he was now the family elder.

"I'm so thirsty," I said, my first words sounding scratched from my throat. The combination of thirst and dryness from the intubation was a parched combo. "Can I get something to drink?"

Mitchel waved at someone who was moving around the room beckoning for her to come to help. The person who arrived looked like a small child in pajamas. I blinked again, trying to get a clearer picture and saw that she was petite but a woman and the pajamas were actually nursing scrubs with Hello Kitty on them. I squinted to read her nametag: V-I-R-G-E.

"How do you pronounce your name," I asked her.

"It's Ver-G, like Virgin without an 'n'." We both snickered awkwardly, although I figured for her this was a routine exchange. "I'll be your recovery nurse here in the ICU."

"I'm so thirsty," I said again, this time hoping she was someone who could actually do something about it. I could barely part my lips.

Virge handed me something resembling a sponge on a stick. I wasn't sure what to do with it, which must have been obvious from my expression because she quickly added, "Just suck. It's all I can give you for now until we're sure all your systems are a go."

I sucked with wild abandon, like a newborn first finding her mother's breast. When the sponge was dry, Virge told Mitchel to dip it into a cup of water and let me have at it again. The only other time in my memory that I have felt so needy and dependent was in the midst of natural childbirth, wailing like an injured hyena with each contraction, begging the unborn baby within me to make its debut and get out of my body. Now again I felt fragile and reliant and it hit me that my recovery would be a process of learning to let go. No matter how Type-A I might be normally, I wasn't driving the boat this time. I had to let my body decide how this would go.

With my thirst quenched I could focus a bit more on the space around me. Tiny lights blinked and undulated from the machinery, each piece of equipment measuring out some element of my vitality: heart rate, respiration and, most importantly, the sound of the blood passing though the new microvessels in my chest.

"Let me show you how the pain medication is delivered," Virge said, gesturing toward one of the various cords trailing across my covers with a red button at the end. "Just keep that next to you and push the button whenever you feel pain. Okay if I check your vitals real quick before I get out of your way?"

Virge eased through the basics taking my temperature and checking my pulse. Then, she pulled back the covers and I got my first glimpse into the war I had just fought. The entire area from my collarbone to my rib cage was covered in an extra large bandage. At the top of the bandage two thin black wires peeked out. Virge grabbed ahold of the wires and plugged them into a machine behind my head. Dr. King had given me an overview of what would happen in the surgery so I knew they were the Doppler monitors. The wires were connected to 1-mm probes implanted within the "flaps" of tissue that had been harvested from my abdomen and moved to my chest to form breast mounds. The probes would stay in place for the first few days to monitor the blood flow through the newly created blood vessels in my breasts. Dr. King had stressed that "flap failure" occurred most frequently in the first 48 hours after breast reconstruction surgery, when the tissue isn't getting enough blood flow. A faint "ub dub" sound, like tiny horse hooves galloping under my skin, were the truest sign of surgical success.

It seemed like hours waiting to hear something. Everyone fell silent opening up the space for the special noise that meant I was okay. Nobody made eye contact, choosing to stare blankly at the space above my bed. I could hear the clock ticking time away. Then suddenly the noise we were hoping for. It was the same echo I heard during my pregnancy ultrasounds. No other sound could be so sweet, then and now. Such a small resonance, yet it made the surgery feel worthwhile. My heart lifted and for the first time I was filled with a feeling of redemption.

"Let's check the other side now," said Virge, bursting my little bubble moment of happiness. She switched the wires and we waited again. Knowing what to expect made the time seem to pass even slower than before.

"Can you give me a cough?" Virge asked. "Sometimes that helps us hear the sound better."

I knew it would hurt to cough. Even the slightest movement made me wince from the pain in my abdomen where I had been cut from hip to hip, but clearly Virge meant business. Besides, I wanted badly to hear that noise again, so I gave a weak excuse for a cough and sure enough the "ub dub" was there.

"Sounds good," Virge said, her simple words offering huge relief. "I'm going to get out of your way now. Anything I can get you before I go?"

"How about that drink?"

Virge gave a light laugh. "You're going to be a fun one, huh?"

"Or maybe some ice chips," Mitchel said, knowing me well. "It was the thing she was most excited for, that and the pudding she is hoping you will offer."

"Hospitals have great ice chips," I said, sending myself into a painful chuckle. Here I was, in the ICU, clinging to machines and gadgets that support my life, and the thing that I was most excited about was frozen water. Silly for sure, but the light banter gave me the feeling that everything was falling into place. Sure, I was hopped up on painkillers, which probably helped. But I had just given breast cancer a swift kick in the chest, and for now I was celebrating my health with ice chips.

Unfortunately, the ice had just barely melted by the time the party was over.

CHAPTER 30

TWIN PEAKS

Out of the 24-hour post surgery woods, I left the constant care and whitewashed atmosphere of the ICU and was transplanted into what appeared like an exclusive San Francisco suite. As I was wheeled into my room I could hear the theme song of the 70's sitcom The Jefferson's, "Movin' on Up" in my head. The first part of the room was replete with couches and a few chairs, and giant bay windows, which were fully functional, allowing for fresh air, not something usually associated with the stale atmosphere of hospitals. Paintings hung on the walls, and there were coffee tables, and a TV. The next room was a more typical hospital room but made more humane by the beautiful two-sided view of the city. Mitchel and I couldn't stop looking at each other and gasping. We didn't want to ask too many questions and get booted. Mitchel did check in with the administrator on our floor to make sure there wasn't a mistake that would mean a move and also to be assured that there was no additional cost for the swank treatment. Even the nurses seemed surprised by the space, as if they did not usually treat patients there. But it seemed that Steve Jobs wasn't here having cancer treatment, Joe Montana was done breaking bones, and none of the Grateful Dead members were rehabbing, so the VIP room was ours.

Everyone who entered the room commented on its grandeur, but sadly, I barely even noticed it. My body felt cut in two, like I was the magician's assistant in the "Sawing a Woman in Half" trick gone terribly wrong. From my waist down I felt like I had been run over by a Mac truck, and I couldn't feel much of anything from my belly button on up.

My body was tethered by tubes and wires in a strange version of medical S&M. My right hand index finger clamped to a tube connected to a pulse oximeter monitoring the level of oxygen in my blood. My legs were covered in pressurized elastic stockings that pumped tight and loose every few minutes to prevent blood clots. A pain catheter was wired into my abdominal wall at the donor site and two sets of drains hung like plastic grenades from under my arms and to the sides of my abdominal incisions. The final tether, a catheter, that transported my urine into a bucket under the bed.

Each day started at the crack of dawn with a "sharp shooter" in a white lab coat, carrying a plastic container filled with empty tubes, band-aids and needles to poke me with. Every few hours through the days and nights, a new nurse would come in my room to take my temperature, blood pressure, and pulse, and empty any fluid in my drains. It was a constant influx of people parading through my room. There were RN's and CPN's, techs, therapists, and MA's, each with a unique role to fill. I tried to remember each one by a certain characteristic—their shoes, the stickers on their name badge. Some that made an extra effort in their care I gave nicknames, like Jamba for the guy at the cafeteria who made me special smoothies each morning or Flexi for the physical therapist who helped me move my legs so I wouldn't get bedsores or clots. My surgeon always came in a flurry, with barely a glance at my sutures and wounds, like his hospital rounds were holding up his golf game.

Day One Post Surgery was going pretty well. I was able to keep up the façade that I was on vacation in a hotel when Mondabe, a sweet medical assistant from Eritrea, came to help me with my toileting and bathing. She was an older woman, with few teeth, and a limited English vocabulary, but the gentlest demeanor as she told me stories of her homeland while tenderly rubbing a rinse-less shampoo through my bedheaded hair. I especially appreciated that she didn't bat an eye when she pulled back my bandages to rinse the skin around my incisions.

One nurse, who I named Wheezy, came in every few hours to measure my success with a contraption called a spirometer that helped to re-expand the lungs after surgery. I found the thing frustrating, and told her that more than one time, but she kept at me, telling me that it was necessary as a way to avoid pulmonary complications that can occur after a long operation, so I complied.

By Day Two of my recovery signs of life began to return. I got myself up and into a chair, ate some solid food, and began to feel a bit more like a human—sleepy and loopy, but more in the world than not.

It became clear that I wasn't going to break free of this glamorous prison until I hit some benchmarks like keeping my temperature down, walking around the hospital floor, and making a bowel movement. My singular focus became walking. I knew I could do it. I came into this strong, fit, and young. Yet it seemed a very long distance from where I was lying in bed to somehow placing my feet solidly on the floor. Mitchel played to the fact that he could tell I was antsy to move and suggested I give it a try when my favorite nurse came on shift.

"First thing is to get your legs free," Eileen said as she unplugged the pulsing leg shackles from under my bed. "You need to scoot your bottom as far to the side of the bed as you can and then swing your legs over the side."

"What did you do yesterday when you got off shift," I asked her, both as a way to stall and because I wanted to remember that there was a real world outside my door.

"I'll tell you when we are walking around the hallways," she said, not letting me off easy. "Take it slow. It takes a little while to let your blood adjust after lying in bed for so long."

"She has a hard time taking anything slowly," Mitchel chimed in.

"I should be in pretty good shape. I teach spin classes in my regular life," I said, as if it was a cardiovascular badge of honor. Indeed, I believed I would be racing around the hospital in no time, but really my body felt like dead weight. This wasn't going to be easy. I needed some inspiration to help me move so I stared at the 5x7 photo of my daughters eating a snow cone in Hawaii that was sitting on my bedside table. I looked at that photo all of the four minutes it took to scoot my body to the edge of the bed. But just this effort had my breathing labored. Trying to catch my breath I started to have a familiar light-headed feeling.

"I'm getting that white thing," I said, knowing that Mitchel would understand. The last time I had it was in Peru at 12,000 feet altitude, when I ran back to the bus after peeing on the side of the road, and passed out right into Mitchel's arms.

"She gets this," Mitchel said, concern in his voice, trying to warn Eileen of what would come next. All I could do was hope that they would both know what to do because the whole room went white. All sight, sound, and consciousness shrouded in the overwhelming sense of nothingness that I get when I pass out.

"Raychel, Raychel," Mitchel's voice was calling me out from this empty place.

I came to fresh as can be sitting in a chair next to my bed like nothing had happened. I looked down to see that the catheter and other wires were still attached to my body but now stretched and pulled to their full extension, but I didn't recall getting there. After I settled a bit, Eileen and Mitchel helped me shuffle back to bed defeated and nervous for next time.

A few hours later we tried again, this time with Melissa, the nurse with the blue and black checkered Vans. I was more nervous given my last failed attempt, but this time we had liftoff. The walk around the hospital ward was a challenge. I felt like my stomach was tied to my shoulders, so I crouched awkwardly. Slumped over like a hunchback, I slowly shuffled my feet thankful for the smooth floor. Mitchel was holding my right arm and kept asking if I wanted to stop and take a break, but I wanted to make use of the momentum I had, so we kept going. Everyone at the nursing station gave me an overly toothy smile, or a hearty thumbs up. The praise felt out of balance with the level of accomplishment, like the way a new mom claps for her baby that smiled because it passed some gas. I tried to feel successful, but for a fitness instructor who could easily teach a grueling hour-long spinning class and not be out of breath, this just didn't seem like much. After two laps, I was ready to be back in bed.

The next day I woke up feeling bright eyed and bushy tailed, ready for another spin. Success and a good night's sleep behind me I braved the walk with only Mitchel helping me get upright. This time I made it a few steps toward the door before I slumped into Mitchel's arms and came to sitting next to him in my hospital bed.

While fainting spell #1 went down with only a note in my chart, #2 meant it was time to call in the big guns. I had not seen my surgeon respond so quickly. He was up in my room within an hour and ordered a special blood draw. When the blood tech arrived, Dr. King whisked Mitchel out of the room. When they returned together it was Mitchel's face that looked pale.

"Dr. King thinks you should have a blood transfusion," Mitchel said. I could tell he was trying to make his voice sound calm although the look on his face gave away the truth. I was freaked out as well. Having come of age during the dawn of the AIDS epidemic, the prospect of having someone else's blood pumping through my veins was fear inducing. Dr. King explained it to me, or really to Mitchel, since I couldn't take much in. They would type my blood and run compatibility tests – this would take a few hours. Then a nurse would do the exchange at my bedside. Each unit would take between one and half to two hours to go in and I would likely need about three units – so this would be a whole day affair. As if I had a choice, Dr. King shoved a clipboard at me and asked that I sign the consent form.

Mitchel and I spent the hours watching my new blood slowly trickle into my veins, making up stories about the people whom the blood belonged to, what qualities of theirs I now had running through my body. We also made a ton of phone calls to folks giving them this most recent update. Luckily, a family friend who had a transfusion during part of her treatment for ovarian cancer assured us that this was the way towards feeling better.

And I did feel better...for a day.

CHAPTER 31

CUPCAKES

By Day 4, things were looking up; I was moving around better, out of the hospital gown and wearing my own clothes, which had me feeling like I was ready to put on my kicks and walk right out of there. I even started to make plans for a birthday at home with my girls in a couple of days.

Dr. King was even in a good mood when he rolled into the hospital for a rare visit, with a visible skip in his step." Things look good with your blood," he said. "You should be out of bed and racing laps around this place today and if you hit all the other marks, we can get you going home."

Home, I thought to myself. The word sounded wonderful swirling around my brain. Home meant being with my girls. Home meant I was on the mend. Home was where I could heal. I luxuriated in these glorious thoughts and didn't notice Dr. King lifting the various layers of gauze bandages off my chest.

"See that little blister right there?" Mitchel asked, but it was clear from the look on Dr. King's face that indeed he had noticed it, and that he wasn't thinking it was such a good thing.

Dr. King explored the area a bit more with his gloved hand, and a few "hmm's" and "huh's" escaping his mouth like extra breaths. Then he set my bandages back in place and asked Mitchel to join him outside the room for a moment to have one of their chitchats that I was becoming used to. Anxiety was creeping over me. It never meant good things. The first time they left to talk like this was in the ICU after surgery upon complaining that I didn't have feeling in my left arm. Dr. King had looked me in the eye and told me it would be fine. Unbeknownst to me he had taken Mitchel out of the room and told him perhaps it was a carpel tunnel kind of reflex and I might need surgery to regain feeling. "She's left handed," Mitchel had said. "That could be devastating." But we learned then, that surgeons like to solve things with more surgery.

"I'm not sure what that blister is, but I'm worried it could be a slow growing infection. I want to go back in there and check on the flap," he said, like it was a routine procedure, and after a brief conversation on the nuts and bolts of how this next surgery would go down, he left Mitchel, dumbfounded, to break the news.

The build up to the first surgery had been so prolonged and focused—months of planning, organizing, and working out both physically and emotionally to prepare. This time however, without an ounce of pomp and circumstance, I would go under again the next day. No prep, no fanfare, just like that. I really couldn't believe that after the eight hour surgery I had already endured there was going to be more. I was more frightened about going under this time—maybe because the first time it was by choice.

The next day a nurse came into my room and didn't even put me on a gurney. He just rolled my bed out of the room, down the hall, and into an elevator to the operating room, more distance than I had traveled in days. I was a real pro at the pre-op procedures except for my pesky veins that continued to refuse IV's as all qualified personnel tried and become sufficiently frustrated. They even called in the head honcho and had the anesthesiologist himself poke at me until he found a vein he liked and soon enough I was in surgery number two.

"So, did they find anything out?" I asked Mitchel, as soon as I came to. I was on my game this time.

"They didn't really find out much," Mitchel said, shielding me from the finer and scarier aspects of what he knew to be true. "The good news is that the flap looks strong." I could tell Mitchel was withholding a bit, but we both knew that keeping our perspective as hopeful as possible was one of the largest keys to my healing and success.

He looked tired. Indeed it was a hard situation for a guy with sleep issues even in the best of slumber situations; the hospital chair bed and constant in and outs of nurses through the night meant little rest. Add to this Mitchel's concern about what was happening with me and the lack of control he could exert over the situation, and sleep was even more elusive. Due to pain meds and an anesthesia fogged brain I was thankfully immune to what was going on around me.

Dr. King made it seem like a relief that there was nothing notable with the flap, but I felt concerned with not having any explanation for the blister that was growing bigger every hour across my breast. My concern was validated a few hours later when a man with a bush of auburn hair walked into my room and asked, "Are you Raychel Adler?" I assumed from his shirt, tie and slacks that he probably was not a doctor. Maybe a social worker I thought, or, after examining his glasses, pinched up face and overall disheveled appearance, maybe a scientist.

"I'm Dr. Slovak," he said, coming to my bedside for a handshake. From close up I could now read his nametag, Dr. Ernie Slovak, Infectious Disease.

My brain did a double take—*infectious disease.* Yep, I read it right. We hadn't had one of these before. Dr. Slovak introduced himself to Mitchel who looked as surprised as I felt. My experience of what infectious disease looked like came from the scene in the movie *E.T.*, when they bubble wrapped the house to create an isolation chamber and everyone is walking around wearing masks and breathing apparatus and keeping specimens in ice coolers.

"Dr. King informed me that the surgery didn't specify a reason for the symptoms you are experiencing." I noticed he didn't say "on your breast" and he didn't seem to be able to look me in the eyes, which usually indicated they had something bad to say.

"So, given that he did not do a biopsy..." the doctor kept right on talking but I cut him off.

"Excuse me, but did you just say he didn't do a biopsy?" I was trying with all my might to not go ballistic at the moment. I must be misunderstanding what he was saying.

"Uh yes, that's right. I'm not sure what happened, but no, there wasn't a biopsy. Now we have to decide how to proceed. Clearly you're experiencing an infection and we need to decide what the best antibiotic to cover all our bases is."

Dr. Slovak went on to mention the various options we could consider. He preferred an IV antibiotic. They were the strongest and they could monitor me well since I was in the hospital anyway. There were several types of antibiotics as well, but the best in this situation he suggested was a broad-spectrum drug that could combat both susceptible and resistant strains of staph infections.

Mitchel, trying to make sense of all the options, asked Dr. Slovak, "If she were your wife, what would you suggest she do?"

"That's a no brainer; I would give her Zyvox," he said, "I would give it to Obama if he needed it. Expensive but the broadest spectrum we can give."

Within hours I was hooked up and on my way to kicking this bug, hopeful that this was the final turn I needed to take to bust out of the hospital. I was anxious to get home and I was dying to see my girls so much that it hurt. Though he knew it was not what I wanted, Mitchel suggested we make a plan for my birthday the next day. He got into my hospital bed next to me with a pad of paper and we began to plan my hospital room party. The one non-negotiable was the guest list. Besides Mitchel and Joel, who were already there, the guest list only had two other names: Marley and Ruby.

When originally scheduling my surgery I had settled upon November, giving myself the holiday season to be home and heal. But then Lisa's life seemed to be quickly coming to an end, so I decided it would be best to reschedule. The pain of making a decision in the face of Lisa's death was excruciating. I knew I would need some time to grieve, but also urgently hoped to do the surgery before turning 36, Lisa's age at first diagnosis. So, I pushed it as close as I could and planned to do the mastectomy the week before my 36th birthday. I figured it gave me enough time that I would be out of my hospital gown and celebrating my special day at home surrounded by my loved ones.

But March 30th had arrived with little to no indication that I would be home soon. My mom instinct told me to have the party somewhere else. I didn't want the girls to see me surrounded by wires and unfamiliar machines. It would be better to see me sitting up, in my own clothes, and as normal looking as could be with all my holes and bandages and pasty skin.

Mitchel suggested that the Family Visiting Room was well suited for a party. I had not ventured yet besides passing the sign on one of my agonizingly slow walks through the halls. I noticed everything on those walks. I could tell you details along the long hallways, like where they stored the medical equipment, how to reach the closest fire extinguisher and the name of the artist that made the origami collage tree across from the elevators.

My main priority before swapping places was to change into my own clothes. A lesson learned from this experience: if you want to get back to feeling like yourself while still stuck in the hospital, put on your own clothes. It worked wonders for me. I picked out a pair of black yoga pants, a supremely soft rose colored cotton v-neck tee (my chest had become sensitive after the surgery so good fabrics were paramount) and my favorite black hoodie and put together an ensemble that managed to look decently cute, while sufficiently covering all my bandages and bruises.

There was no rush for me to get to the waiting room since the girls weren't there to notice my sluggish gait, or that I was still having trouble stretching my abdominal incision to stand up tall. Better to save some energy for the return walk to my room with the girls. Hopefully adrenaline would fuel me at that point so I could keep up with Ruby as she raced up and down the long hallways on her two year old pokies. Marley would probably stick more by my side, taking in the surroundings and trying to process it all.

Mitchel and I stopped at the nurse's desk first and the excitement for me was palpable. We had spent a good amount of time with these folks and we had shared so many stories about our girls. One of the nurses said she would come down to the Family Room to bring them pudding.

The Family Room was large and bright by hospital standards and did not have the distracting buzz of my hospital room, a cacophonous mixture of the static of fluorescent lights and beeps of hospital equipment. Floor to ceiling windows let in natural light and the furnishings were more like home: couches, game tables, a flat screen TV, and even a puzzle of the Eiffel tower 60 percent complete, waiting for someone to come finish it off.

I got myself situated on the largest couch in the room so there would be space to comfortably cuddle with the girls, and we made a plan. Nancy, our friend who was driving the girls to San Francisco, would call when they got off the Bay Bridge. Nancy and her daughter drove my girls and my sister-in-law Jill who was staying at our house in Davis. Mitchel would meet them all in the parking garage and on the way up to my room would remind the girls to be gentle with me. I was worried about what I would do when I saw them. I might not be able to keep myself from squeezing them tight and covering them head-to-toe in kisses.

Indeed it was a wonderful reunion full of kisses and cuddles, ice chips and chocolate pudding. Seeing the girls invigorated my resolve to heal up and go home. Love is such a powerful force in the universe.

And the icing on the cake was this: I was given the greatest birthday gift possible—Nurse Jen came in to deliver the pudding and also the good news. I would be released to go home the next morning.

CHAPTER 32

BEACONS

I woke at early dawn, the sun not yet even reaching my window, anxious to get the day started. It was my homecoming. Mitchel was still asleep in the sofa chair in the corner of the room. That night we would have our bed. It was nice to watch him sleep while the sun slowly started to rise over the city. Streaks of pink and blue clouds almost seemed to draw arrows in the sky, pointing south, where a few miles away, I had been born, 36 years before to that very day. A sense came over me that this was exactly where I was supposed to be.

Seeing my girls the day before really reminded me of what I had done. I saw a future in all of us I hadn't seen so clearly before. Together we would pave the way to something better ahead.

Compelled to write down all the thoughts swirling in my head I groped around my bedside table for a pen and the only paper surface I could find, a tissue box. On one side of the box I wrote out my thank yous. First to Mitchel for the special kind of love we shared.

All of this could even rock the boat of Mike and Carol Brady and their bunch! As we have duly noted to each other a few hundred times this past week - we promised "for better or for worse"- and you did not even begin to falter at a time of worst's. You have shown everyone around us what it means to hold up a loved one.

My offering to him was to throw a Hawaiian luau in his honor. Celebrate my health, his birthday, and the hope of now having more years to celebrate together.

My thanks continued to pour through the pen, next on to my community.

It will take my lifetime to express my deep and humble gratitude for the multitudes of gifts you have bestowed upon me. The emails, calls, cards, FB posts, flowers, cute new button/zip down clothes, plants, chocolates, foods, tender help fanning me or tying my hair back....this list, truly is endless.

After a visit from my girls yesterday that eased my aching for them, I feel I have actually had the most amazing, life-and-love affirming birthday of my life. We are still a bit in the woods about what lies ahead - and whether or not my Double D left boob will ever deflate...but at the beginning of this day, I do know that thanks to each and every one of you - I really can do anything.

My birthday blessing brought me to the last side of the tissue box where I wrote this toast:

And so, in a birthday tradition of toasting my guests, I raise my glass to you:

May we live with big, honest and open hearts

May we appreciate big and small - everything from the power of love, to the life-giving force of breath

And may each of us have many opportunities to enjoy love, laughter, health and happiness together for many years to come!

With no more space on the tissue box I decided it was time to wake Mitchel up. I wanted to spend part of my farewell day with him, and there was strangely a lot to do before we could leave. Besides a bunch of medical tests before they would give my discharge notice, Mitchel needed to pack up all our stuff since I couldn't help, and Dr. King would be by later to go over post op instructions.

Finally, by 2 pm they agreed to let me out. As the nurse assistant rolled me out into the spring air of San Francisco I took my first breath of fresh air in days. As I started to tear with the sheer joy of fresh air the ironic smoker in her hospital gown stood around the corner. We drove away toward home and health with a mantra of "no flap failure" in our minds.

TETONS

"Helped are those who find something in
Creation to admire each and every hour.
Their days will overflow with beauty and
the darkest dungeon will offer gifts."

-Alice Walker

CHAPTER 33

GRAPEFRUITS

Coming home was both a relief and a challenge. It was wonderful to be in my house with my family, but my healing wasn't progressing, which made me feel far from San Francisco and my surgeon who might know what was happening. Each day the blisters and strange skin lesions stayed or, in some cases, looked worse. Mitchel took on a new role as my personal nurse, donning blue latex gloves night and day before inspecting my left breast with a flashlight. While ooze, blood, and medical decisions that seemed dire weren't his thing, Mitchel cared for me with his usual gentle, loving way.

Our bathroom looked like an operating room, every surface covered with sterile scissors, gauze, tweezers, and steristrips. We started a list that had the date and time and then a rating—same, better, or worse, and wondered each day if we should go to our local ER or just email pictures to Dr. King. Marianne Sandrock, a good friend and neighbor who was also a nurse, became my personal home health aide, helping me change my dressings, bathe and check that things were progressing.

I had to manage four drains coming out of my body, so I devised a set-up wearing a belt that is normally used to clip a racing number to your body when participating in a marathon or triathlon. When I raced my half marathon to celebrate my body before my surgery and wore the belt to hold my race number, I never thought I would be using it again, and especially not to hold bloody grenade shaped medical devices close to my waist. But it worked to keep the drains out of view from my squeamish little girls and tucked away from potential vectors of infection.

Several times a day I measured the output of each drain by squeezing them into little measuring cups, hoping that their total brought me close to the 30 ccs or less of fluid in a 24-hour period that would mean I could uncork my drains. I scribbled these measurements next to long lists of the times of day I had last taken a pain pill or my antibiotics.

Although my scars did not seem to be healing and there was some seeping fluid discharge, we remained hopeful that things weren't getting worse and convinced ourselves that with time, the wounds would heal.

A call from my breast surgeon helped to ease some of the stress of my recovery. Her message said that she had been very thorough about how she harvested my breast tissue and really felt she had gotten as much as she could—and the best words of all, that my pathology report came back as clear of all cancer. There were no cancer cells found in my breast tissue. That one message made all of the struggles I was having worth it.

I was, however, really challenged by an incredible amount of lethargy and fatigue. This was a whole-body-and-mind kind of tired. The only other time I had felt this exhausted was at the beginning of my first pregnancy. Newly with child, but not yet having shared this with my colleagues, I was worried they would notice my eyelids sagging at meetings or that I barely got up from my desk all day. One day I was so tired I needed a midday nap, but didn't know where to go so that I would stay unnoticed, and wound up in my car asleep in the backseat. Our temporary office building was located in the red-light district of Sacramento, so we shared the neighborhood with many transients and questionable looking characters. I shouldn't have been so surprised when a manly looking woman knocked on my window and asked if I was all right. Shaken by the interaction I wandered back into the office and decided it was time to tell my office mates that I was pregnant so I could move my lunchtime napping to the break room.

Now again I was tired to the bone. My friend, Denise, who is a Reiki specialist, had come by my house to do a cleansing session on me, in hopes of getting my positive life energy moving again. She mentioned that the body takes a while to sleep off surgery and all the medications, and that combined with the healing that needed to happen I needed to take it easy on my systems and get some rest.

But this tired was about more than sleep. I was moving slowly and my thinking was sluggish.

Mitchel, now covering both of our parenting duties while I healed, was putting our girls to sleep, when Marley hit on a philosophical truth.

"Daddy," she said with a bit of questioning in her voice, "I think mama is like a Tortuga."

I didn't hear how Mitchel responded because I got lost in what she had said. My Kindergartener was commenting on my metamorphosis from active Super Mom mode, to being like the most stereotypically slow creature on the planet. Marley was aware of my connection to these creatures, but now she was naming something bigger, my transition toward my true center.

While many little girls dreamed of swimming with mermaids or dolphins, my visions were of swimming through the deep blue, guided by sea turtles. I had always been drawn to their simple yet wise demeanor. I associated them with being supporters, community builders, and peacemakers, flexible and life giving.

My link to these creatures seems to have started when I was 8 years-old when I fell into a manmade pond of giant sea turtles at the Kahala Hilton Hotel on Oahu. We stayed there every April, while Pop did business with some Hawaiians who co-owned a strip mall with him back in California. I believe this business relationship was one of Pop's most brilliant professional moves, to seal a deal with people who lived in our dream vacation spot.

Every time we returned to the Kahala Hilton we would find a basket, overflowing with tropical fruits and macadamia nuts in our room. They would set these gifts on the sitting room table that we would soon push aside to make room for the rollaway bed, creating my Hawaiian beach bedroom.

Early risers, my parents would get up, have a simple breakfast, and start a tennis game, before I awoke from my tropical dreams. My mom would leave me a note by my bed telling me where to find them. As a parent now, this is not something I would allow my own children, but back then the world felt safe and sweet, and I enjoyed the thrilling adventure of making my way through the Hawaiian jungle of hibiscus bushes and towering fragrant tuberoses.

My sea turtle baptism came as I was running along a narrow path from the hotel to the outdoor/indoor restaurant by the beach where my parents were having breakfast. I must have taken a small misstep, deep in a daydream of the sweet bread and jellies awaiting me, because next I knew, there I was, sitting in two feet of water in a pond full of giant sea turtles. I wasn't scared. I was a good swimmer and I knew from previous time spent watching these creatures that they moved very slowly. I knew I could get out of there before they got to me and believed they would be gentle with me if they ever did catch up.

As I got older I connected with turtles on more levels. As a self-declared vegetarian at the age of 12, I was drawn to the creatures' vegetarian ways. As a swimmer, I loved that they were both land and water dwellers as well. As a Grateful Dead fanatic, I loved the Terrapin Turtles. And then, in college, as a budding anthropologist, I uncovered yet another dimension of these creatures as I became drawn into the study of creation stories. A common thread was the belief that a tortoise had been sent by the "creator" to establish a place for creatures to stand on top the waters of Earth. In another story of myths surrounding our geographical beginnings, it said that the original conglomeration of continents in our universe, the Pangaea, resembled the outline of a turtle.

The final hook for my turtle obsession came through the words of the book, "*The Temple of My Familiar*," by Alice Walker. In the first chapter of the fifth section is "The Gospel According to Shug." Delivered in three unbelievable pages Shug's Gospel described an ideology that I could buy: hook, line and sinker. Truly words I could live by. The art that marks the new chapters in that section of the book is an African woodcut of the top of a tortoise shell. I knew this was the symbol I wanted to make a part of my body forever.

One foggy San Francisco summer day I went to the Marina district with a Xerox copy of the turtle shell design in my hand. I walked in to Tattoo City, owned by Ed Hardy, and in two hours my tattoo was placed solidly between my 3rd and 5th chakras, representing the centers of Feeling, Emotion and Thinking. These energy zones also represented the elements of water and air, much like the land and water loving habits of my turtle friends.

My tattoo is the external symbol of my internal compass. It gives me a center and strength that I have called on many times in my life and like the sea turtles, it was guiding me now, through this most challenging of times.

Even Marley could see it. "Slow down, let yourself heal, remember your inner core," the art on my back reminded me.

some serious pain, so I had to work hard in order to remember what he was saying so that I could recount it to Mitchel later that night.

A few days later we returned to the same hospital and to the wonderful cast of characters we had met there only a few weeks before. The third time was the charm—the surgery was successful, and Dr. King had done a biopsy, so we would hopefully have some answers soon about why all this was happening.

The first couple of weeks, things seemed to be moving in a positive direction. When the biopsy results came back it showed that I was suffering from a MRSA (Methicillin-resistant staphylococcus aureus) infection. Within days of getting on my fifth round of antibiotics, this time Vancomycin, the correct one for my ills, my pain had subsided and I was a lot less tired. The other good news was that the holes under my left breast appeared to be closing up, and my right breast was almost completely healed. I felt so confident in this new direction that I told Mitchel he didn't need to come to my next appointment with Dr. King. My dear friend, Ann Murray Paige, a breast cancer warrior herself, drove me to Marin to see Dr. King in his off-site office. What a great drive that was, jamming out to 80's rock and filling myself with Ann's positive attitude. Sometimes I worried that being around me reminded Ann of the dark side of breast cancer, since we had met when she was only a two-year survivor and my sister was close to dying. But, if that was the case, Ann never let on, that day, or ever, that I was bringing her down.

The lobby of Dr. King's office was filled with people with hand injuries. With no bandage or visible problems on my hands I am sure that everyone knew what I was there for. When a nurse called me back to the room, Ann asked if I wanted her to come or wait there.

"Wait there is good, thanks so much," I said before I was whisked away to the back office.

"I'm so sorry Mitchel is missing this appointment," Dr. King said. "Finally it is good news, things look great. Next time you come in we'll work on expanding that breast a little more, though you're almost there."

I should have learned by then not to hold on to any promises, but it had been a while since I heard anything positive, so I grasped onto his words like a child sucking their first lollipop. I hung onto it so hard that I even overlooked some pretty clear signs that things were not so bright and cheery after all.

One month later, my friend Holly offered to take me to my next post-op visit since Wednesday was Mitchel's biggest day at work. I dropped my girls off at school and told both of them that the babysitter would pick them up and I would see them later in the afternoon. Holly and I made an afternoon of our trip to San Francisco, stopping in Berkeley for lunch and a little shopping trip at Title 9, for swimsuits of all things. I left my bandages in place and a loose sports bra over my chest as I tried on any bikini top that did not require me to lift my arms to get it on. When I looked at myself in the mirror, I imagined myself healed and how my new cleavage would look jutting up over the top of the 36C cups of the suit.

Holly came with me into my appointment, curious to see in person the mysterious Dr. King I had been talking about.

"How are things?" Dr. King asked without looking up from the notes in his file.

"Not quite as good as the last time you saw me," I said. "It's painful to move from any downward position to being upright for some reason. Is that normal?"

"Let's take a look," he said, and asked me to remove my shirt and sports bra.

Dr. King's face went flat. He put on some gloves, came over to my breast, gave it a squeeze, and then flopped down defeated onto his examination chair.

"We've got to take the breast," he said. "You've got a virulent infection."

The wind was whipped out of me and I had a moment of time standing still. All I could hear were his words over and over again, "take the breast, take the breast, take the breast."

"What do you mean?" I asked as soon as I was able to compose myself. "When do I need to do this? Oh my god, I can't believe this is happening!"

"I'm admitting you now," he said. "I want to get you on IV antibiotics as soon as possible. I'll call over and see how quickly I can get into the operating room."

Suddenly, the pace of my whole mastectomy experience amplified. There were all the months I had taken to choose a procedure and then a doctor. The many days spent in the hospital waiting to be released. The long arduous days at home on the couch, unable to do even a small portion of my daily activities. And now, in a single instant, my worst-case scenario of being left with no breast was being thrust at me with no time to consider options.

Dr. King left the room to make his call, and I started to cry. Holly tried her best to console me, but all I wanted was to talk with Mitchel. I checked my watch and it was a few minutes after 2, so I knew he was in session and wouldn't answer. I left a long voicemail, sobbing as I told him the news and begging him to call me back. When he called after a long half hour, I was across the street being admitted. We made a plan for what to tell the girls and when he would get to me. A few minutes after telling Mitchel that I loved him and to give the girls big hugs and kisses for me, I entered the twilight of anesthesia for the fourth time in two months.

The first day after my surgery I didn't want to look at myself in the mirror, convinced that if I didn't see myself without a breast, it wasn't true. I went to the bathroom to change, turning my back to the mirror, so I didn't have to look. Mitchel was concerned about my anxiety and denial and suggested we consult with the on-site psychiatrist. Begrudgingly I obliged, mostly because I knew they were not going to release me from the hospital if I couldn't change my bandages, which meant looking at my body. The psychiatrist offered me some Ativan to help with my nerves, and a good faith prescription that I would be brave and take a look.

I went to the bathroom alone. First, I unbuttoned my shirt, letting it hang to the side so I could see myself with my entire chest wrapped in bandages. The right side was clearly more raised than the left, but the gauze that was covering my left side offered the illusion that I had a bosom. Slowly I pulled away the layers of bandages, looking more toward the mirror than down at my chest, and I was staring at my non-breast. The skin folded into itself, filling the hollow cave where my breast had been with rolls of skin and my areola—a flopped soufflé. It was terrifying, and I quickly began to wrap myself with clean bandages to cover it up. I had looked like I promised, but that was all I could take. With the bandages in place it was easier to accept that the surgery was a necessary evil in order to let the infection out of my body.

This was my new, lopsided normal.

Leaving the hospital I made a vow to myself that I would not return. There were too many negative memories wrapped up in that place, the trauma of this last experience was the final straw.

I spent the first few days at home trying to figure out how to get dressed with my new shape, picking loose dresses and button down shirts, and wearing multiple layers to cover up for what wasn't there. Knowing the summer weeks ahead were going to be filled with swimming pools and sundresses, I sent away for a mail order booby, a silicone prosthetic from Makemeheal.com. Although a decent fill-in, a plastic removable breast does not function in the same way as a natural one does. My wardrobe choices became determined by what kind of breast pocket or neckline the top had. It had to either cover up the granny style bra that could hold my prosthesis, or offered elastic at the chest so that I could just stick it in and skip the bra.

The further from the surgery, the more I was able to find some humor in the situation. The best laugh was at the gym when my prosthetic boob didn't move with my body the way righty did. Watching myself in the mirror during boot camp class I wasn't sure if I should laugh or cry as my left boob slowly made its way to my belly button by the time we were done with jumping jacks.

A moment of shining glory with my foob (fake boob) was just two months after surgery when I completed a triathlon, and as I crossed the finish line, I pulled my plastic boob from my sports bra and held it over my head in victory.

A visit from Mitchel and the girls at the hospital after I lost my breast.

CHAPTER 35

BOULDERS

Surgery to place another implant couldn't happen until my body had shown its ability to remain infection-free for three months after stopping antibiotics. Nobody wanted to touch me with a ten-foot pole after they heard I had a MRSA infection. I even had to take antibiotics before I got my teeth cleaned.

To fill the time, I began to visit with breast surgeons closer to home this time. I was taken aback by the response I got from the practitioners I interviewed. Most of them were very curious about what had happened, behaving as if my chest was a science fair project or mystery to be solved. I was particularly aghast when one doctor asked what he was looking at. When I explained what had happened, and about the original skin and nipple sparing techniques that were used, he suggested that he start fresh and remove what had been saved. I left his office quickly.

I settled on a good-enough surgeon, Dr. Anderson, because although his techniques were more old school than some of the other doctors I'd seen, his demeanor was gentle, and he was an upstanding member of a Davis church. Really, I let that influence me. After my experience with Dr. King, both in being so far from home and also feeling like I was just a case number and not a person to him, the idea of being cared for by someone who sat in the pews with members of my community was comforting. So, I went under the knife for the fifth time to place a fresh expander in my chest to prepare for an implant.

The expander was a whole new experience. Each week, for 12 weeks, I visited Dr. Anderson's office for a "fill" where two tablespoons of water were shot into my chest with a long aspirating needle, slowly expanding my breast like a water balloon.

The process of expansion was more painful than anything I had experienced so far. It was a good thing that each session made me feel more and more like myself physically, because the anticipation of pain made it hard to show up. By the second fill I learned to take Ibuprofen before my appointments in anticipation of the pain that would come as the chest muscles were stretched to allow for the expander to enlarge. The throbbing radiated into my back each time. Sometimes I could tolerate the full amount of expansion, other times I had to stop short. The pain was worth it because each time I left the doctor's office, I looked more and more like an even-chested woman.

The other challenge of the expander came as I got closer to full, and my left breast was hard as stone. My breast felt like a weapon, ready to bonk you in the head, or hold up a bank. And then there was trying to sleep, which had been an issue since my first surgery, but was actually worse with the expander because I felt like the Princess in the Pea sleeping on a boulder.

My Barbie moment arrived during my sixth surgery when I got an implant. My original choice of the DIEP flap was centered on my preference to go natural. Now that I was going the implant route, I picked the next best thing, silicone, because it most clearly mimicked the feel of human fat. Plus, Dr. Anderson had explained that if a silicone implant were to rupture it would most likely stay in place, whereas saline would change shape and size. He also assured me that the current silicone was not the same as the toxic kind I had heard of in the past.

It was a relief to get that boulder out of my chest, but disappointing that the new implant didn't make me look like a

Hollywood starlet. Mine was dimpled and creased, shaped like a heart lying on its side. My nipple was left of center, pointing due east rather than straight ahead. Still, I was able to feel some closure. Medical urgency was gone. Any surgery I had from this point forward would be chosen revisions. Or so I thought.

CHAPTER 36

FOOBS

For the one-year anniversary of my last Thanksgiving with Lisa, and to celebrate that I was done with surgeries, I invited Dylan, Elliott and Bruce to come to California to be together for the holiday. It would also be good timing for us to do the Jewish custom of unveiling Lisa's headstone. I wanted the gathering to be a celebration of Lisa's life, and my new lease on living. It felt important to acknowledge that while so much had been lost, there was also great bounty to be appreciated. I was thankful that through my health challenges I had learned so much about what I valued in life. I had found a great appreciation for the resilience of my body and mind and the strength of my vitality. I had given my family and myself a new future. I had given my girls a chance to have a mom without breast cancer. I had taken the breast cancer target off my chest. And perhaps most importantly, I had added a small piece to the puzzle of medical genetics, which I believe moved us one step closer to a cure.

I was thankful for the small things: Ruby's sweet warm breath on my skin when she got in bed next to me in the morning, Marley's eyes shining as she read new words in her "I Can Read" book, the sound of our dog, Monty, lapping up the water in his bowl.

I gave thanks for the big things too: that I was able to do a triathlon two months after major surgery, that Mitchel found me sexy, even with just one boob, and that the biopsy of my breast tissue after my mastectomy showed all tissue to be normal.

My gratitude extended to new friends who'd shown me that it is never too late to make friends for life, and to old friends who continued to stand by me over and over again, with energy and generosity that felt like it was still the first time.

As well as plan our Thanksgiving meal, and what I would say for grace, I made a playlist of songs to have at Lisa's unveiling the next day. The first song I picked was by India Arie, the musician who had inspired Lisa over the years and headlined the last concert I went to with my sister. The words to the song were apropos, and I decide to offer them as the blessing over our Thanksgiving dinner: "It doesn't cost a thing to smile. You don't have to pay to laugh. You better thank God for that. Stand up for your rights. Keep shining your light. And show the world your smile."

Surgery and breast cancer were behind me, and I was ready to celebrate.

Lisa meets her hero, India Arie, when we go to her concert. My first concert was Hall and Oates when Lisa took me (I was about 8 years old). This was our last concert together.

CHAPTER 37

GARBOS

If I were a scriptwriter and could write the story of my life that would go on the big screen, the next few months would have looked very different than the reality. The camera would pan to my home, beautiful rays of sunlight streaming in through perfectly washed windows, my children with beaming smiles as they walked next to Mitchel, who is holding a chocolate cake covered in birthday candles, one of which is shaped like the number 1. As I blow out the candles, my family calls out that I make a wish.

"I already have all that I want," I would say in this version of my life. "One year ago today you were in my hospital room celebrating my birthday – and today, we are here. I am cancer free, healthy, and so very happy to be here with you all."

The next scene would cut to me on the streets of Downtown Davis, walking into Urban Tattoo, and telling one of the overly pierced employees that I want a new tattoo. A girl named Casey, with blue spiky hair and an eyebrow piercing, would etch a beautiful tattoo onto my left breast—a heart with wings, designed in the style of a Mexican milagro. The camera would artfully flash a shot of my chest, the tattoo transforming my dimpled and morphed breast into a beautiful work of art.

But my life didn't develop that way.

In fact, instead of the tattoo, the only body art I ended up getting is the heart with wings that Marley drew on my cast.

The beginning of the story started out on course. Dr. Anderson had suggested I wait two months after he placed the implant before I did anything that could potentially impact the surgical site. That timeline put me at March, a great season to celebrate since it was also my birthday, and the one-year anniversary of my first surgery. In honor of this, I planned a week's worth of festivities, beginning with a day trip to Tahoe to ski with my friend Natalya.

Natalya had recently returned to work after a ten-year hiatus to have and raise kids, and now had a very full time gig with the California Pesticide Management Program. The bright side of her work was "Furlough Fridays," which, though a bummer in terms of state economics, was not a bad way to return to the workforce since it allowed for trips like this. For me, the get-away was a chance to do just that, get, away. Not in a bad way, but rather for a good change of pace, and to do something for fun with a good friend.

During the car ride I heard about Natalya's work and her thoughts on life as a full-time employee and mom. We talked about our kids, about play date protocols, and landed in the parking lot of Northstar Ski Resort around 11:00 am. After getting out of the car and stretching, we chose our gear and clothing, deciding to pack light so we wouldn't have to get a locker. I sat on the edge of the tailgate and grabbed my right ski boot. As I lifted it up, part of the heel fell onto the snow. Bending down to grab the part, I noticed a screw on the snow. Flipping over the boot I saw that only two of the four screws were in place.

"Look at this," I said to Natalya. "What the heck am I supposed to do?" I held up the fallen piece and showed her the bottom of my boot.

"That's strange. Did it just happen?"

"As far as I can tell. I just picked it up and the part fell off. What am I going to do, rent some boots? That's so annoying. We'll have to get a locker after all since I have to walk up there with my shoes on."

"Hold on a sec. I have a little MacGyver part of my personality," Natalya said. She walked to the front of the car, reached into the glove box, and came back with a mini screwdriver.

"Impressive. I didn't know that about you."

Natalya proceeded to use the screws in place to secure the heel part back onto my boot. While she worked, I packed my Camelbak with tangerines, trail mix and a few slices of cheddar cheese. Natalya put some ak-mak crackers, a wedge of parmesan, nuts and chocolate into her hip pack.

Northstar had really changed since I was there as a kid with my family, more built up with restaurants, shops and even an ice skating rink. As a child, the greatest thrill was going into the hot tub at our condo surrounded by snow. The other shift was that now everyone was carrying snowboards. Natalya and I joked about how old school we looked with our skis surrounded by all the 20-somethings with their boards. Still, we were happy to be among them.

A quick gondola ride took us to the main part of the mountain where we took a few runs on gentle slopes to warm up. It was a beautiful day—clear skies, great sunshine, not too many people, and it felt invigorating to be outside being physical with my body.

As a kid the only time we went skiing was on sun-shiny days like these in March and April. I would wear a long sleeve t-shirt and sunglasses rather than goggles so I could come back to school with raccoon eyes and everyone would know I went skiing. It was standard protocol to leave one's ski tags dangling from your coat zipper, a collection of cool experiences. This day was bringing back memories of those sweet times.

After an hour or so on the front side of the mountain, we decided to move to a new section called the "Back Side" via a chairlift called the "Backside Express," worth a giggle or two. We were skiing runs with names like Sierra Grande, Rail Splitter, Challenger and Burnout—all black diamond shoots off a blue-square main run.

Getting hungry and ready for a break, I asked Natalya if we should make "one last run" before stopping for a rest.

"Oh, don't say that. I'm too superstitious," Natalya said.

"Me too, actually." I replied with a laugh. It seemed a funny side of ourselves to be sharing. "I heard someone say that people get in car accidents more frequently after a long drive, when they're just a few miles from home," I said, realizing that I was only making matters worse. Luckily the conversation was cut off, as it was time to get off the chair.

I followed Natalya over to Sierra Grande, a run that traversed the top of the mountain, and we decided to branch off to Challenger. Natalya headed down the top portion of the run with me behind, and then she stopped at the ridge before the next decent, where a group of people were mapping out the view ahead of us. "That parking lot over there is Alpine Valley," one woman explained to her friends and now to us. "And Squaw Valley is over there." She gestured a little farther along the horizon.

"It doesn't get much more beautiful than this does it?" I said to Natalya and I felt it. I was healthy, able to be physical, and with a great friend enjoying the day.

Natalya nodded in agreement. "The only thing better would be if you got some of these skis." She looked down at her feet in admiration, and knocked a small bit of snow off of them with her pole. "Okay, should we get going and be ahead of these folks?" Natalya gestured at the people gathering around us and then pointed her poles down the mountain in a gesture that suggested, "After you."

I took off over the little precipice and skied down half the next face before I started to trip. It felt like my right ski was getting stuck in the thick smoothie-like spring snow and then one leg fell from under me and the other flew into air in the opposite direction. I heard something that sounded like the cracking of small twigs to make kindling for a campfire. The pain was instant—a burning, pulsing and throbbing throughout my ankle and radiating into my shin.

Natalya recounts that I took two or three tumbles on my way down, but I just remember sliding down the mountain, unable to stop myself. I looked uphill and saw one of my skis streaming toward me like an arrow to finish me off. Along with everything else, I would wind up with three stitches in my left thumb from grabbing my ski before it hit me in the face.

Natalya was quickly by my side. "Are you getting up or are we calling someone?"

"Calling someone," I said, knowing that this feeling in my body meant I was not getting up.

The group that had been looking at the view with us before skied up, and asked if I was okay.

"No, we need someone to call for help," Natalya said.

In the next few minutes, which felt like hours due to the pain, several others skied by and Natalya asked all of them to make contact with the ski patrol. While we waited, Natalya managed to get my other ski off and I lay down on the snow.

Two girls in full body ski team suits skied by slowly and one of them called out, "We'll have our coach radio to the Ski Patrol."

It must have worked because soon enough a ski patrol guy wearing a red Northstar jacket was standing over me holding a little notebook. I read his nametag: Dave, from Carson City.

"What kind of skier are you?" Dave asked, starting a barrage of questions.

"Were you wearing a helmet?"

"How long have you been skiing today?"

"How fast were you going?"

"Do you own your skis or did you rent them here."

From his questions I wasn't sure if he was assessing my pain and injury or covering Northstar's butt from any future legal woes. He even made me sign the bottom of his report. My signature was wobbly from how my hand shook from the pain.

Eventually, Dave did a manual check for head, neck and spine injury, and then he opened up his supply bag and started to situate the materials he needed to set my leg for the ride ahead.

"Can you give me something like ibuprofen?" I begged.

"We can't. I'm sorry. We aren't certified to give out medications."

"Can my friend give me some?"

"They really prefer that you don't take anything until you are in the ambulance."

Ambulance. I hadn't considered that I would be going anywhere by ambulance.

"What's the alternative?" I asked.

"Well, we have a clinic here on the resort," Dave said, "but it isn't that well equipped to handle what you have going on here."

I wondered what it was I had "going on." Dave had barely glanced down at my boot, so I was surprised he had already made an assessment. "And they can't give you pain medication there either. Based on your pain scale, and what I can see about what's happening, I think we should get you to the ER."

The pain was snowballing and made worse by all the movement from Dave trying to fit on the air splint.

"Can you straighten your leg at all ma'am?" Dave asked, and then called into his walkie-talkie for backup.

I looked down at my leg positioned awkwardly. Slowly and with great deliberation I was able to place my leg onto the splint.

Another ski patrol guy showed up and helped me scoot toward the sled.

The first leg of the journey was by toboggan. I was zipped up in a yellow plastic cocoon, cringing in pain at every bump and shift we made. There was one skier pulling the sled and another at the back, "cracking the whip." This meant that he was pulled along in the back, gaining momentum as we moved downhill, and then he would ski out in front of the sled and pull us along with a yellow piece of rope to get some speed going uphill. When we got to more challenging terrain, we met up with a third ski patrol guy on a snowmobile. They attached my sled to the snowmobile and continued along a much thinner and steeper path in the back woods.

My brain was pulsing and I could barely hear a thing by the time we pulled into a driveway where an ambulance was waiting. From what I could see outside of my toboggan cocoon, we seemed to be in the middle of nowhere, like they were hiding me from all the excited skiers in line to buy their tickets for a day of wonder. A woman in a toboggan with a grimace on her face is not good for sales.

The ambulance doc asked more of the same questions I had answered with Dave, but focused on my health rather than who was to blame for the accident. Thankfully he quickly got me loaded into the ambulance and hooked up to IV medications. Aided by morphine and his "second line of attack" drug, we made small talk about spinning classes and Davis, where he had lived during his adolescence and early adulthood. At one point he dropped a bomb by using the word "surgery" as a possibility for me, which jolted me out of my druggy daze.

"That's not going to happen, right?" I asked.

"It's hard to say, but this is the best place to be if that is the case."

Indeed, when I was wheeled into the Tahoe Forest Health System ER, I could tell that Mr. Ambulance Man was right. One entire wall in the examining bay was covered in different sized crutches, like they were art decorating the wall. *These people see a lot of broken legs*, I thought to myself.

Natalya was by my side as soon as they brought me in. While I had my wild snow ride, she has skied down the mountain, collected my things, gotten her car, and driven to Truckee. The doctor explained that we would do some x-rays and see what was happening with my leg. They would give me a little "happy juice" to relax me while they removed my boot and then casted up my leg.

I looked at Natalya and asked, "Can you call Mitchel now?"

"Sure thing," she said as she picked up the phone. I was anxious about whether or not he would pick up, and also about the disbelief he would experience when he heard what happened.

"I'm so sorry, sweetie. Are you in a lot of pain?" Mitchel asked.

We talked briefly until the nurse was ready with my happy juice. The next moment of clarity I can recall was back in the exam area with a cast up to my lower thigh.

"You are most likely going to need surgery," the doctor said. "We can set you up to do a consult here with our surgeon or you can go home."

"I'll be going home," I said, not missing a beat. I didn't want to be away from the girls and Mitchel having surgery again.

"Okay, we'll get you fitted with crutches and then you guys can get on the road. I'll give you a prescription for pain meds that you can fill at the CVS across the highway," he said to Natalya.

Natalya pulled her car around to the front of the ER in the ambulance bay and a few people helped maneuver me out and into the backseat.

"Here's a CD of your x-rays to show whoever decides to treat you. And here's a bag in case you get car sick."

I guess that on top of broken legs, the good people at the Tahoe Forest ER also know a heck of a lot about the combination of IV painkillers and the curvy ride down the mountain because within a half hour of driving, I used the bag.

Two days later, on March 22nd, and two days before my original surgery anniversary date, I had surgery number seven, to put 14 screws and a metal plate into my right leg.

Perhaps this real life drama would actually make a better movie than the one I had planned.

It was, quite literally, the start of a new leg of my journey.

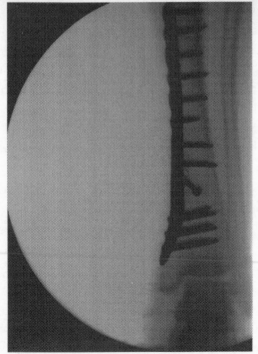

Another setback. 2010

CHAPTER 38

HEADLIGHTS

Of everything I had been through already, healing from my leg was the hardest. Part of the challenge was that I didn't choose it. Plus, I was completely dependent. The requirement not to be weight bearing for three months meant that I could not walk or work out, but it also meant no driving. I devised all kinds of ways to get around, my kids' favorite being rolling around the lower level of our house on a wheeled desk chair. I paid our babysitter to drive me to the grocery store and zipped through the aisles on the electric carts they offered customers that I had never noticed before.

Eventually, when I could drive again, and soon thereafter, when I was walking without crutches, life began to get back to order. Before I knew it, two years had passed and life in most cases returned to its normal pace and ways. While the experiences and challenges I had faced informed the ways I led my life, I enjoyed having more and more space between what life had been, and what it was becoming. But then, as life will do, it threw a curveball my way. I realized I could never get away from my past and that, perhaps, I didn't really want to.

Coming home one day I grabbed the mail on my way in the house. At the top of the pile was a card from Elizabeth Thorley, my sister's financial planner. Usually Elizabeth's office, Cross Bridge Financial, sent me Lisa's monthly statements, and occasionally some tax documents I needed as executor of Lisa's estate, but this document did not come in a business-sized envelope.

Inside the house, I put my workout bag and groceries down on the counter and opened the envelope. Pulling out the card, it was a picture of a piece of cake with legs and arms that said, "Our Clients are the Best," and on the inside, "And you take the cake." At the bottom of the card, written by hand it said, "Happy 56th Birthday Raychel!"

I was breathless. Not that at age 40 I was afraid of aging, but in that moment my sister and I had become the same person, our lives merged in that one sentence. It was true in so many ways. As executor of Lisa's estate, I was in command of all Lisa's assets, and how her legacy would be doled out to her sons. But the deeper level of our lives coming together in this way was the opportunity Lisa's misfortune allowed for me. I was now living life for both of us.

When Dylan called me a few days later on Lisa's actual birthday, I assumed he was calling to touch base, as we liked to do on special calendar days. But when he started talking, it seemed he didn't even realize it was her birthday.

"Hi Auntie Ray, I have something exciting to tell you." Then without skipping a beat, he blurted out that he had been offered a job in Palo Alto and was moving out west. The company that hired him, Apigee, was located a quarter-mile from where Lisa was buried.

I got goose bumps thinking of how Lisa's spirit was still guiding us. She was there with me every time I got dressed or undressed. The years after Lisa's surgeries she had told me, "You don't want to see my breasts, Ray Ray. I'm like Frankenstein." I caught a few glances when I was helping her into a dress or in those last days when she couldn't get dressed on her own, but basically she had kept her scars hidden.

Since my surgeries, my breasts had worn a burqa as well. The only time they were unveiled was in the shower, or if Mitchel turned out the lights during lovemaking so we could enjoy some skin-to-skin contact, without my feeling self-conscious. Otherwise they stay covered up.

Ruby was okay with seeing me naked. I think it was easier for her to accept my new-fangled booby since she didn't have any memory of what it looked like before. One time in the shower she said it looked like my left breast was winking at her. Maybe it was Marley's age, or her deep-set fear of all things medical or gory, but she didn't want to look. Her fear, I imagine, developed when my chest was bandaged and full of tubes and fluids. I hid things even more when I had a crater chest and wore a plastic prosthetic. In the pool and hot tub, although our family was inclined toward au naturel when we were at home, I started to wear a swimsuit, I stopped showering with Marley, and became the mom who was always in a bra. Just like Lisa had done with me, I mostly kept old lefty under wraps.

While I didn't often reveal my physical state, I began to expose my emotional world more. I started to worry less about people's reactions when I told them about my surgery and choice. I became a coordinator for FORCE, starting a local Sacramento chapter, and began speaking publicly about BRCA and my reconstruction experience. The more I exposed the intimate parts of my life in words, the more I felt ready to open up physically.

It started at the second FORCE conference I attended. I was really enjoying myself. These were my people, especially someone I met the first night named Jennifer Nance Gooch. Jen and I had a very similar story and some very comparable messed-up boobs. Jen had been through 15 breast surgeries by the time I met her, and was the first person I'd met who had a rougher go of this than I had. While I wished a different story for both of us, we bonded over infections, flaps, implants, scars, sex, and more. When we both admitted that we wanted to be brave and take part in the Show and Tell room on Saturday night, we decided that we could do it if we did it together.

A FORCE conference is like no other professional conference. While it does offer a full day of research-based presentations, when the sun goes down it becomes ladies' night. Jen and I and a few friends started the evening off with a hosted poolside party and then enjoyed a more intimate "Pure Romance" party in someone's room. After some great laughs over edible underwear and chocolate flavored lube we felt we were ready to brave the Show and Tell room.

It was like the Take Back the Night of breasts—a roomful of women wearing vests cut from paper medical gowns, drinking wine and eating sushi as they perused a buffet of breast reconstruction options. Jen and I stayed clothed for a while, getting adjusted to this bizarre world of boobs. After a little bit it felt stranger to be in my clothes than I imagined it would be to take my top off. So I did. The experience was terrifying, especially answering questions about my reconstruction and what happened as people looked at my boobs. The worst was when someone apologized for what had happened, a look of disgust on their face that suggested how horrifying the view was. But in the end, I would say the experience was redemptive and certainly bonding for Jen and me.

When I got back from the conference all fired up I told Marley about the pedometers we had all been given to make sure we were getting our walking in. I explained to her that research had found it beneficial for those with a BRCA mutation to use fitness as disease prevention. Talking a bit more, we came up with a great goal for her. Recently diagnosed with Celiac disease or at least a high gluten intolerance, Marley was not growing taller, which on her small frame was a challenge. She was looking for a way to get a bit more exercise in her life and the pedometer was a fun game. Her goal became to walk 10 percent more steps a day than her baseline 10,000, by her 10th birthday, three months later, and raise money for FORCE while she was at it. That meant 1,000 more steps a day.

A local reporter caught wind of Marley's efforts and asked if she would do an interview and photo shoot. I wasn't sure how it would go, if I would answer the questions and fill in the data, or if Marley could handle it herself. It was a wonderful mothering moment when I saw my baby was now a girl, with a great head on her shoulders and a giant generous heart at her core. Marley stepped right into the interview and told the reporter what she'd learned about the benefits of getting exercise as prevention even for genetic cancers, and that it sounded like a fun plan to try to walk more and raise money for a cause that was near and dear to her.

I was beyond the proud mama that day, beaming that this was the way my daughter was facing what lay ahead. It wasn't until the reporter asked her if she inherited the gene that I got nervous—not because I thought Marley didn't have the answer, but because I knew she did, and that made my stomach quake.

"I have a 50-50 chance," she replied, with so much hope in her voice, I realized that, while I was scared for her, she was not. She was facing this head on, and with an outlook of gratitude that her mommy didn't have breast cancer.

The baton had been passed, and this relayer was coming in strong, head held high, looking toward a bright future.

The night, after the interview, Marley said it would be okay to look at my breast.

Marley Moves fundraiser for FORCE

EPILOGUE

There is a Buddhist story called "The Farmer's Luck." It starts with an old farmer working his crops, and his horse runs away. The villagers hear this sad news and say, "Such bad luck," to which the farmer replies, "Maybe." But the next day, the horse returns, bringing along two additional horses. His neighbors all exclaim, "Such good luck," to which the farmer again replies, "Maybe." The story continues with the farmer's son trying to ride the untamed horse and breaking his leg after being thrown. And the farmer replying to the villager's cries of "Such bad luck" with his usual "maybe." The next day some Army officials come to the village to draft young men into the army, and while many of the village boys are recruited, the farmer's son, with his bad leg, is passed over.

The truth is we never know what will happen when one door closes.

I have become a walking, talking, breast reconstruction handbook. Directions and warnings are written in my scars. On each breast, a cut in the shape of The Eye of Horus, the ancient Egyptian symbol of protection, is placed to guard me from the ills of breast cancer. At the base of my belly, is the shape of a smile, stretching hip-to-hip, happy that my once villainous belly fat now heroically fills out my upper body curves. And gracing my shin, is a fishhook, the final catch after a year of barbs.

These marks show where I have been, and also the growth and repair that I have done to heal. When I look at my scars I see the life I have created and the path I am showing to my daughters and to many other girls and women in the world.

I can't deny that there are times I wish I could have my old breasts back and feel I would do anything to get rid of my dimpled breast and the scars on every part of my body. And yes, I have moments when I wish I didn't experience burning sensations on my chest. I am sometimes sad that I will likely never ski again, and that when I run now, my right leg feels like a pogo stick, rigid and bouncy at the same time. Of course, I fear the day when Marley or Ruby turns to me and says, "Will this happen to me?"

But all of this only reminds me of the choices I have made, and the life I have created for myself. For all that has been taken from me, so much has also been gained, by what I have gotten off my chest.

I will probably always continue to worry about getting cancer—melanoma from all the sun I have gotten or lung cancer from a bit too much fun in college. And not wanting to be the dummy that cut off her breasts and ended up with ovarian cancer means there will be more surgeries in the years ahead. My plan is to have an oophorectomy when my IUD expires in two years. And from what I have heard, I can expect surgical menopause to bring unwanted symptoms like hot flashes, trouble sleeping, dryness and lack of desire.

Within ten years I will need to change out my implant, and I may decide at some point that I am done with my implant, and try for a flap again, maybe they will take it from my hips next time.

Also in the future is the decision of when I should talk to my girls about being tested. Sometimes when I go into their bedrooms to give a final tuck of their sheets and kiss to their face, I am hit by the contrast of how peaceful they look and how stressful this legacy of breast cancer can be on a life. I am their mom, and I want to take away pain, discomfort, and fear, not add to it by what I have given them. I want them to keep the looks of innocence on their faces for as long as possible.

Still, I am well aware that my issues are not their own, and that they will have different and more vast options for how to live their lives in the face of what we know about their risks. I hold hope that the science of how we treat genetic disorders and how we are able to defend ourselves from the threat of cancer will evolve in their lifetimes. Perhaps in the future, testing positive for a genetic mutation will offer an opportunity to take a vaccine that will get those cells doing their cancer fighting job again.

It is my biggest hope that my daughters may grow not to see their breasts as enemies, but rather view them with the same dream-filled, starry-eyed wonder that I once had as a child, stuffing my bras with tissues, or imagining themselves as mermaids in seashell brassieres. In the same way as I have taken my own path, different from my mother and sister, they too will have a chance to live a beautiful, unique, life in asymmetry.

Let them imagine coconuts.

Acknowledgements

My deepest love and appreciation go to my sister Lisa. She will never read these words - but I believe she died knowing she made a profound difference in my life. Thank you Lisa—my twin separated by 16 years, for giving me the gift of life.

Mom and Pop: Although one of you passed me this gene, you also gave me the basis for being the positive, resilient woman that I am. While you were both taken from me too soon, I am glad you were spared from knowing that you had passed this along to me.

To my husband Mitchel, always my champion and greatest support, I offer my profound gratitude for sticking with me through all of this. You are a gleaming example of what it means to be a loving caregiver. When people read about my surgeries in this book, the story they will not get is what happened to you during that time. Like the fact that you didn't for a second let me catch on when you were told by my surgeon that I had a life-threatening infection. You have always supported my decisions about how to face my genetic status, even when the ramifications meant adjustments for you as well. You have nursed me, dressed my wounds and shown me your sweet loving eyes through all of it. I'm so happy that life ups are so much more than the downs, but in any case, love that I am on this journey with you. Thank you for all of it.

To my daughters, Marley and Ruby—thank you for being a big part of the reason why I want to live a different life then my sister. Any choice I can make to improve my health so that I can be part of your lives for longer is the choice I want to make! I love you both to the moon and back - for infinity times. This book is meant to help make a brighter future for you - and maybe even for my grandchildren some day.

Thank you to my brother Joel for being a pillar of love and support throughout all of this – and by that I mean all of my life! Hope these stories resonate for you too.

And to Dylan and Elliott... I have always felt like your mom-aunt, long before Lisa was gone, but even more so now. As she gave me life I promised her that I would be there for you for all of your lives. I hope you feel it. Thank you for letting me tell parts of your story – I hope you find comfort in remembering Lisa through these stories in the same way that I do.

And to all the wonderful people who welcomed me, a newbie, into the writing community with open arms. Each of you has been instrumental in my writing process. Please accept my gratitude for holding my words so close to your hearts and for helping me learn and grow with such tender care toward my words and journey. To my first writing teacher, Don Schwartz, and the great folks of his Davis Art Center classes, particularly Owen Aptekar-Cassels and Henry Anker, two then high school students, who taught me so much about great writing by sharing theirs. That class is also where I met Adam Russ, who became my writing Yoda over the next 4 years as this book came to life. Adam never gave up my inability to remember simple grammatical rules and you can thank his great editorial skills for getting endless drafts into this shape. Also, Rae Gouirand and the good folks I encountered in her group, Brenda Miller and the participants in her workshop, and members of the various writing groups I was a part of while writing my memoir- particularly Lisa Slabach, Susan Walker, and Denise Hoffner. Last, but certainly not least, a humble thank you to Alan Titche, who stepped in at the final hour (a mistake on my part), to bring you this grammatically improved and cleaned up manuscript.

The list of family, friends, doctors and nurses that all created the beautiful rainbow hammock of care for me through all of this is impossible to innumerate, but I do believe that when you read this you will know who you are, and I offer you my deepest gratitude. To all the folks that came over to my house and offered up a gift of their generous hearts - the kindness was extraordinary. What I loved most was seeing how each person decided to show their care, from shaving my overgrown legs, to a newish friend who drove me to San Francisco for a post-op visit and stood next to me as I learned I was about to be admitted into surgery where I would lose one of my reconstructed breasts. When I broke my leg, another friend who I'd only met a few months before when our daughters started kindergarten together, came in and cleaned out my refrigerator- tossing old salad dressings, wiping the shelves— all without my ever asking her to do anything. And particular thanks to my neighbor, Marianne Sandrock, who came over daily to check on me and my wounds and offer her comforting nursing skills during my first days home from the hospital. I am blessed to be surrounded by the most amazing rainbow hammock of a community – both far and near! I could never have done it without all of you. The light in me bows to the light in you.

A hefty thanks to Maude Blundell, the person who first told me about my mutation and also the person I credit for bringing me to FORCE. Maude was my genetic counselor, and often times I would think about Maude and think how very hard it must be for her to work with patients as they discover these hidden elements of their lives. Yet she did it so well for me, with equal amounts science and kindness.

While there were many great nurses, PA's, assistants, phlebotomists, and doctors, the one that stands out the most is Dr. Engy (named changed), the surgeon who removed my breast tissue when I had my mastectomy. One of the things I really appreciate about Dr. Engy is that I feel confident that she worked tirelessly to remove as much of my breast tissue as was medically possible. I can't tell you why, but I really trust this to be true, and I appreciate it. I only met her once before the surgery, and the second time when I was already under the knife, but her words, "Your pathology came back without any sign of cancer," were the best thing I have ever heard in my life.

To the amazing women at the helm of FORCE (Facing Our Risk of Cancer Empowered), Sue Friedman and Barbra Pfeiffer: You would never know that these two women run an international non-profit by the way they treat you. In my case, they welcomed me into a whole new world. Because of FORCE I have never felt alone on this journey.

Which brings me to all my BRCA sisters— the best darn club you don't want to be a part of: Madeline Boyle Bernal, Caryn Joy Schmit, Rachel Savage Householder, Jennifer Nance Pitts, Beth Jaeger-Skigen, Sandra Lear Cohen, Lisa Schlager, Lisa Edwards, Teresa Dillinger, Sonya Zindel, Lita Goldstein-Poehlman, Teri Smieja, Kathy Stilego and so many others I have connected with over the years thanks to Facebook groups, FORCE boards, and conferences.

And last but certainly not least, to Loran Wyman, Cathy Berman, Ann Murray Paige, and Susan Quintana...breast friends for life!

This story belongs to all of us.

About the Author

Raychel Kubby Adler lives in Davis, California, with her husband, two daughters and their dog Chewbarka. She holds a Master's in Public Health, is a certified Wellness Coach, teaches cycling classes, runs a conflict management/physical education program, and writes a blog on wellness, parenting and breast cancer.